From time to time, God brings a< recognize as coming from Him. As I special blessing and guidance on this wc written on spiritual growth, I believe th rare books that speak equally to laymei. ... ...misters alike. I wholeheartedly urge every believer and pastor to prayerfully read this book and experience the life God intends for all His children.

DR. GREGORY FRIZZELL
Prayer and Spiritual Awakening Specialist
Baptist General Convention of Oklahoma | The North American Mission Board

This message is life changing! God has given Dr. Ted Kersh the ability to bring the Word of God to life in a simple and understandable, yet profound way. While reading *The Blessed Life*, I found myself wanting more of Christ in every area of my life. The Sermon on the Mount will become very personal through this book, and you'll understand how living the blessed life means living a life that is never apart from the Lord.

ROBIN MARSH
Television News Anchor | Oklahoma City, Oklahoma

Ted Kersh has a pastor's heart that sincerely wants his people to receive all that God has to give them. In his book, he carefully and gently opens up one of the most beautiful passages in the Bible. You will be encouraged and challenged by what unfolds.

DR. RICHARD BLACKABY
President, Blackaby Ministries International
Co-author of *Experiencing God, Revised Edition* | *Spiritual Leadership* | *Fresh Encounter*

This book is a fresh and dynamic look at one of the most beloved texts of Scripture. While sound in exegesis and interpretation, the strength of this book lies in its fresh application to life in the twenty-first century. Dr. Kersh makes the ancient text come alive with powerful illustrations cut from the fabric of everyday experiences. Some books add to knowledge; this book adds value to your life and journey with Christ.

DR. ANTHONY L. JORDAN
Executive Director-Treasurer | Baptist General Convention of Oklahoma

In this "more-is-better" world, we need to regain God's perspective. Too many of us have bought the lies of the "prosperity gospel," and we've forgotten that only the way of the cross leads home. If we want to truly live, we should look at the life and teachings of our Lord. He modeled and manifested the abundant life God intends for each of us.

Jesus pointed the way to that life, particularly in the Sermon on the Mount. His words are counter-cultural, but the truth found therein is the key to an abundant and fulfilled life. The world has it all wrong. Jesus got it right. Even within the church today, we need a course correction. We need to regain a heavenly perspective on life, priorities, self, and others. We need to rethink the basic issues of life, such as marriage, family, and our witness.

Ted Kersh has done us all a favor by writing this book. His study of the Sermon on the Mount is biblically sound, and his applications to life are right on target. If you will read and embrace this pivotal study, your life will be enriched. You'll find that you are increasingly becoming the salt and light God has called you to be. You'll discover that what Jesus spoke almost two thousand years ago still works . . . in any culture, at any time, with any person willing to take Jesus seriously.

MICHAEL CATT
Senior Pastor, Sherwood Baptist Church | Albany, Georgia
Executive Producer, Sherwood Pictures

We all ask God to bless us, but will we follow His path to receive that blessed life? Do we ask God to fill our hands while our fists are tightly clinched? That will never work! Dr. Ted Kersh provides us with a biblical, trustworthy, well-written guide on how to live the blessed life, based on Matthew 5-7. This book should be read—and applied! You will be blessed.

DR. DENNIS NEWKIRK
Senior Pastor, Henderson Hills Baptist Church | Edmond, OK

Even before opening the manuscript, I knew it would be a clear, inspiring work of art. Part of its beauty is Ted's humility and openness to the Holy Spirit for fresh teaching. I fully endorse the author and the book. They will inspire you to persevere.

GARY RICHARDSON
Attorney, Author, and Member of South Tulsa Baptist Church

The Blessed Life

The Blessed Life

Living the Sermon on the Mount

DR. TED KERSH

CrossBooks™
A Division of LifeWay
1663 Liberty Drive
Bloomington, IN 47403
www.crossbooks.com
Phone: 1-866-879-0502

Editorial team: Dana Bromley, Meagan Brooks, Janna Allen
Cover design and illustrations: Kim Hayes

First published by CrossBooks 04/25/2012

ISBN: 978-1-4627-1652-4 (hc)
ISBN: 978-1-4627-1654-8 (sc)
ISBN: 978-1-4627-1653-1 (e)

Library of Congress Control Number: 2012906631

Printed in the United States of America

This book is printed on acid-free paper.

I lovingly dedicate this book to my bride, Jerri. Only our Lord knows the storms she has walked through as a pastor's wife—and she always walks through with grace. She is a lady who understands and lives the blessed life.

And to my children—Paul, Micah, and Rebekah. You are the joy of my life. For many years, you've been a vital part of this ministry, and I thank you for your continual encouragement. Your lives exemplify walking with Jesus. I could not be more proud of you.

To the wonderful people of South Tulsa Baptist Church. Your prayers and encouragement strengthen me daily. I hope you hear me when I say, "I am proud to be your pastor!"

Contents

Foreword

So how *should* a Christian live, really? And what may a true believer expect out of such a life? Those are good questions, so good in fact that our Lord devoted an entire sermon to their answer. The Sermon on the Mount, preached primarily to His intimate followers, but in the presence of a much larger and curious audience, reveals the Lord's heart regarding the lifestyle expected of His followers. "The result," said Christ as He introduced the sermon, "is the blessed life."

Over the years, Christ's Sermon on the Mount has been the subject of multitudes of sermons, a vast array of studies, and countless hours of serious contemplation. In fact, Matthew 5-7 was the first lengthy passage many of us were challenged to exegete as new seminary students. Unquestionably, the sermon's introductory beatitudes, or "blessed attitudes," quickly found their way into the heart of every true believer. Like the entire sermon, they soon became something of a plumb line for the soul, a genuine measure of one's Christlikeness.

Now, my friend Ted Kersh brings us a new and refreshingly insightful approach to the message Christ preached almost two thousand years ago on a Galilean hillside. His gracious and gentle spirit, seasoned with his devotion to the Lord and His Word, enables Ted to write authentically about issues already hammered out on the anvil of his own experience. As his own family and church family would verify, Ted's life, both personally and professionally, certifies the principles so clearly taught in this book—and that is why you will read this book with a sense of confident expectation.

Do you desire a life that is blessed and full to overflowing? Christ makes such a life possible! As you turn the pages of this book, Christ's Sermon on the Mount will come alive. You will quickly grasp New Testament word pictures and illustrations that may have been a puzzle to you. The timeless truths of Christ will become fresh to you in both appreciation and application. I do not doubt that this book's message with its practical, down-to-earth approach will become a resource to which you turn time and again.

You are about to hear the Sermon on the Mount with the ears of your heart and to read it with the eyes of your soul. So, prepare yourself for a life-changing experience as you travel the path toward the blessed life.

TOM ELLIFF

President, International Mission Board | Southern Baptist Convention

Preface

There is something unique and miraculous about reading the Bible. We may read a passage of Scripture so many times we can even quote certain verses. Then one day, as we read those familiar verses again, it's as if we're reading them for the very first time. We find ourselves asking, *Where have I been? How have I missed this truth all of my spiritual life?*

Something happens in that moment. The Holy Spirit takes the Word of God and breathes new life into it. Words that have always been perfectly wonderful words now explode with fresh meaning. God, by His Spirit, allows us to read His Word in a new, life-changing way. It's as if we discover a hidden room in the house in which we've lived for many years—and the room is filled with treasure. That is what happened to me a few years ago, when I began to study and preach from Matthew 5-7. In that section of the New Testament, commonly called the Sermon on the Mount, the Lord was teaching the first four of His eventual twelve disciples: Simon Peter and his brother Andrew, and James and his brother John. These newly called men had seen Jesus perform miracles and had heard Him teach the great truths of God. Now, in this setting (probably the Horns of Hattin, west of the Sea of Galilee), Jesus was training them to touch the world in His name.

While preparing to teach the Sermon on the Mount to the wonderful people of South Tulsa Baptist Church, I grew increasingly excited. God did an amazing work within me as He opened my understanding and unfolded His purpose for preaching this sermon. I shared with my congregation, and now with you, that it's possible to walk through the inevitable difficulties of life with contentment, trust, and a solid witness to the world. That life, outlined in Matthew 5-7, is the "blessed life."

Now, please do not jump to any conclusions, because this is not a book claiming that health and wealth constitute the blessed life. It is far from that—and so much more. *The Blessed Life* is a guided tour through the Sermon on the Mount, in which Jesus taught us in clear practical terms *how to construct God-anchored relationships, homes, and churches that stand strong through life's storms.* What a hope-filled prospect!

This Bible study is spiritual food for all believers, new and seasoned, and it's a tool for pastors and small-group leaders seeking to train others in discipleship, biblical scholarship, or spiritual formation. One way to approach this book is devotionally; for example, invite God to teach you as you read through a section; then take a day or so to meditate on the Scriptures in that section, to delve deeper into the Bible, and to pray about and apply the things God teaches you. A few questions follow every chapter, all designed to help you apply the teaching personally and practically. I hope you'll dedicate the time to work and pray through these, because they will help you prepare for—and even survive—life's storms.

I'm asking the Lord to teach us as we reflect on the marvelous truths found in this wonderful sermon by our Lord. Together, let's learn to live the blessed life.

Acknowledgements

I have so many people to thank.

My assistant, Melanie Ketchum, truly guards my time. Thank you, Melanie, for graciously managing many tasks so well.

Church staff members, each handling a mountain of responsibility, allow me the time to write, study, pray, and preach. I thank all of you.

This book would not have happened without the Lord performing the miracle of placing Dana Bromley in my life. Dana has edited all of this material. As I shared with her early in this project, I am a preacher, not a writer. She has taken the thoughts and words of this preacher and developed a book that is far beyond my ability. Thank you, Dana.

I sincerely thank Tom and Sara Whitwell and Bob and Linda Meyer for encouraging me to write *The Blessed Life*. The manuscript was conceived the moment you said, "Pastor, you should write a book!" Tom and Sara, Bob and Linda, I will forever be grateful for your kindness.

The screen saver on my computer scrolls, "All to the Glory of God." My greatest desire is to glorify God with my life. I pray this book accomplishes that desire. If there is any acknowledgement, it must be to the glory of God.

1

The Blessed Life:
What It Is, and How to Get It

Matthew 7:24-29

Therefore everyone who hears these words of Mine and acts on them,
may be compared to a wise man who built his house on the rock.
—Matthew 7:24

We live in a peculiar world. When many of us think of "the blessed life," our thoughts immediately turn to money and material possessions. We don't have to listen long to television preachers before we hear them express with great gusto that "God wants to bless us" and to give us material possessions. And we hear them say that with enough faith, we will have riches. With enough faith, we'll always be healthy. We can even buy oil, spring water, and prayer cloths that will bring us "special blessings." From all this, one would think that a successful Christian is the one who is healthy and wealthy, living a life filled with only bliss, wonder, and happiness. The only thing wrong with that teaching is, it's just wrong. Certainly, it's a long way from the life the apostle Paul lived. Listen to the following description of the great apostle's experience in serving the Lord:

Five times I received from the Jews thirty-nine lashes. Three times I was beaten with rods, once I was stoned, three times I was shipwrecked, a night and a day I have spent in the deep.

I have been on frequent journeys, in dangers from rivers, dangers from robbers, dangers from my countrymen, dangers from the Gentiles, dangers in the city, dangers in the wilderness, dangers on the sea, dangers among false brethren; I have been in labor and hardship, through many sleepless nights, in hunger and thirst, often without food, in cold and exposure.

Apart from such external things, there is the daily pressure on me of concern for all the churches. (2 Corinthians 11:24-28)

Does Paul's life as a follower of Christ sound anything like the blessed life promoted by many contemporary preachers and teachers? I do not wish to be unkind, for that's not the purpose of this book, but I do desire to be honest. Surely, Paul lived a blessed life; yet, the life he lived was a life of difficulty. In fact, he told his young friend Timothy, "Indeed, all who desire to live godly in Christ Jesus will be persecuted" (2 Timothy 3:12). If, according to the apostle Paul, godly living includes persecution, then it appears the blessed life must be something other than an easy life of following Jesus.

I believe Jesus taught us through the Sermon on the Mount (Matthew 5-7) the ultimate truth of what it means to live a blessed life and what that life looks like in our daily lives, its benefits in life's difficulties, and much more. Let's listen in as Jesus taught the truth of the blessed life.

What Blessed Is

In the early days of His ministry on earth, Jesus had been teaching throughout Galilee, and as a result, large crowds were following Him. The Scripture tells us that on this particular day, "When Jesus saw the crowds, He went up on the mountain; and after He sat down, His disciples came to Him" (Matthew 5:1). Jesus "sat down," taking the position of a teacher, and His first few disciples—the men He had called to follow Him—came to listen. Although a large number of people may have listened to the Master teach that day, it appears that His sermon was not directed to the crowd at large, but to His disciples. It's also a critical sermon for those of us who are present-day disciples of the Lord Jesus.

When Jesus began preaching the Sermon on the Mount, He spoke words that had never before been heard. In a series of statements that we call the Beatitudes (Matthew 5:1-12), He began to talk to His followers about the life that is "blessed."

> Blessed are the poor in spirit, for theirs is the kingdom of heaven.
>
> Blessed are those who mourn, for they shall be comforted.
>
> Blessed are the gentle, for they shall inherit the earth.
>
> Blessed are those who hunger and thirst for righteousness, for they shall be satisfied.
>
> Blessed are the merciful, for they shall receive mercy.
>
> Blessed are the pure in heart, for they shall see God.
>
> Blessed are the peacemakers, for they shall be called sons of God. (Matthew 5:3-9)

Although many equate the word *blessed* with the word *happy*, it seems to me that blessed describes a state of being that far exceeds mere happiness. Two times in the Bible, the word *blessed* is used to describe God.

> According to the glorious gospel of the blessed God, with which I have been entrusted. (1 Timothy 1:11)
>
> He who is the blessed and only Sovereign, the King of kings and Lord of lords. (1 Timothy 6:15)

In some way beyond my comprehension, God is blessed. The people whom Jesus described in Matthew 5:3-9 as "blessed" must then, by definition, be touched not by luxury or wealth or ease, but by God Himself. My friend, the blessed life is a life that has God all over it! To have the strong, guiding hand of "the blessed and only Sovereign" on our lives deems us blessed, a state far better than mere happiness or ease.

The Lord characterized blessed people as gentle and poor of spirit. They are people who mourn. They hunger and thirst after righteousness. Blessed people are merciful and pure in heart. They are peacemakers. Then in a startling statement, Jesus declared that blessed people would be persecuted.

> Blessed are those who have been persecuted for the sake of righteousness, for theirs is the kingdom of heaven.
>
> Blessed are you when people insult you and persecute you, and falsely say all kinds of evil against you because of Me. (Matthew 5:10-11)

You and I have something in common. In life, we all experience difficulties. I do not know what's coming my way tomorrow, but I do know the trials I've already experienced. I know the grief children feel when parents die. I know what it feels like to be disappointed by the people you love. I understand the hurt of being deceived. My wife, Jerri, and I have at times helplessly watched our children go through excruciating emotional and physical pain. To most of us, *blessed* and *persecuted* couldn't possibly fit together in the same sentence—that is, until we experience the strong, guiding hand of the blessed God on us in our most difficult times. Then, at that moment, we can only be thankful that they do fit.

Personally, I feel that I can go through anything if I have the hand of God on my life. What about you? Are you going through some difficulty today? Is something or someone shattering your confidence in others? Is someone you love destroying that love—maybe a spouse or a child? Perhaps you're walking through a confusing or even depressing experience that makes you question whether you'll make it through another day. Are you going to work or school with a smile on your face, but inside you're crying? Maybe you're at a place in life when things were supposed to be easier. Your plan—for the children to be on their own and off your payroll—is not working out. You thought that by now the struggle you're suffering through would be over; but the fact is, you see no light at the end of a very long and dark tunnel.

I have good news for you—*you do not have to be destroyed by the difficulties of life*. You can walk through any circumstance when you are endowed with God's protection and presence. You can survive and live blessed with the hand of the blessed and only Sovereign guiding you and strengthening you.

Now that we understand the deeper meaning of the term *blessed*, let's get to the bottom of Jesus' purpose for preaching the Sermon on the Mount. Read on, as we continue our journey toward the blessed life.

Storms Do Come, So Build Well

When preparing for a sermon, preachers must first choose a text from the Word of God. Once a text is chosen, we then decide how to expose the meaning of that text. Eventually, we will determine not only the meaning of the text but also the purpose of the sermon. We must ask, "Why am I preaching this message?" This process is also true concerning Jesus' Sermon on the Mount. So, to gain a solid understanding of His purpose, I think we must begin at the *end* of the sermon, Matthew 7:24-29.

> "Therefore everyone who hears these words of Mine and acts on them, may be compared to a wise man who built his house on the rock.
>
> "And the rain fell, and the floods came, and the winds blew and slammed against that house; and yet it did not fall, for it had been founded on the rock. Everyone who hears these words of Mine and does not act on them, will be like a foolish man who built his house upon the sand. The rain fell, and the floods came, and the winds blew and slammed against that house; and it fell—and great was its fall."
>
> When Jesus had finished these words, the crowds were amazed at His teaching; for He was teaching them as one having authority, and not as their scribes.

In this familiar passage, Jesus told a parable of two builders and two foundations. It seems that one builder wisely built his house on a rock, while the other built on sand. Storms of equal force and duration raged against each house, and as the story is told, one house stood, the other did not. What's the spiritual parallel? A wise builder intentionally builds on the strongest of foundations—Jesus Christ, who is the perfect shelter from any storm. Conversely, a foolish builder builds with shoddy material (anything other than Christ) that is no match for a storm. The outcome, whether standing or falling, depends on choices made by the builder.

Imagine with me the vastly different experiences of each family. Let's say that a father, a mother, and two children live in each house. Most likely, both sets of parents wanted to build something more than a physical structure—they wanted to build *a home*. After all, a house is merely the structure in which a family lives; the family itself is the real home. I'm privileged to live in a nice house. It's not an unusual house, and it's not especially large, though it is in a nice neighborhood. It's just your basic *house*. Brick with wood shutters. Three bedrooms, a nice den, and a dining room (you know, the room where you never dine). If you enter our house, turn left, and walk down a hallway, there you'll begin to see our *home*. Take a look at the three black-and-white pictures hanging on the wall in stairstep fashion. Within each frame is a handsome couple. These are our three children and their wonderful spouses. Behind you and to the left is our kitchen. There, over the breakfast bar, you'll see a picture of seven children. Now you really see our home! These wonderful creatures are our perfect grandchildren. You see, the house is not the home. The house is only a representation of the real home—the family.

The houses Jesus mentioned in His parable are, in reality, homes, and the mothers and fathers are like you and me. They have dreams. They want the best for their children. Every day the fathers work hard to support the desires and needs of their families. Each family longs for joy and fulfillment. One day, however, everything changes. Unannounced, a devastating storm blows in. The clouds turn to dark gray; the dark gray explodes into an ominous green. The winds roar, and the clouds burst in a torrent of rain. Yet, even in such a storm, one of the houses stands firm. The house next door, however, begins to shake. As the dazed family inside wonders what's happening, the house suddenly lurches as it shifts on the sandy foundation. The walls crack. The ceiling, under the weight of enormous stress, sags low; water begins to soak through the drywall; rain floods into the light fixtures and down the walls. With a sudden flash of lightning, the house implodes in a heap and washes away. But the house is not the only thing that's destroyed. The home itself breaks apart. Dreams die. Plans vanish as quickly as the water rose. The people in this home stagger wounded and confused. In a moment, life turns hard, harsh, and hurtful.

Friends, Jesus was not teaching us about the destruction of bricks and wood. He was telling us about the destruction of a home. But be encouraged—this tragic scenario is not the end of Jesus' teaching. In His goodness, our merciful God did not leave us ill-equipped and uninformed as to how to build homes—lives, children, relationships, jobs—that stand firm in life's storms. At the end of His sermon, Jesus described the home that stood in life's storms—and why it stood.

Wise Builders Hear and Act

Don't you love to get a great deal? A friend of mine came by my office one day in the middle of the afternoon. It was unusual for someone to knock on the outer door of my office, a door that was marked private and opened into the parking lot. As I opened the door, my excited friend said, "Preacher, I've been out looking for a new vehicle. You have to come see what I just bought." Then my friend paused, and I could tell he was about to utter those anointed words every man loves to speak: "I went out this morning to buy a new SUV, but . . . I could *not* pass up this deal!" And with one sweeping motion, he pointed toward a brand new sports car—an amazing, black Toyota Spider. (Here, we see an opportunity for me to obey the commandment, "Thou shalt not covet thy neighbor's car." I failed the test.) Beaming from ear to ear, he continued to tell me about his "great deal."

Friends, Jesus offered His listeners an amazing deal. He told of the blessings that come from listening to His words and doing what He says. In pictorial language, Jesus explained that if we obey the Sermon on the Mount, then we wisely build our lives on a solid foundation. When a great storm comes, when mighty winds blow, *our lives and homes will stand.*

Unlike the predictable spring storms that pass through Oklahoma, you and I never know when a life storm is coming our way. Oklahoma lies in "Tornado Alley." We do have our share of tornados. Most of the time, however, we're alerted early enough to prepare. (If you're a real "Okie," when the storm sirens blow, you head outside to watch.) When alerted, wise people take shelter in an interior closet or bathroom. Not long ago, our son Micah, anticipating a tornado, told his family to take cover in the closet (while he went outside to watch). Creed, Micah's oldest son, excitedly ran to the closet and donned his football helmet. Well, the storm passed with no problems, and that evening, Creed gave us his six-year-old account: "Grammy, Granddad, we got into the closet . . . 'cuz Daddy said a 'big tomato' was coming."

That "big tomato" had been clearly detected on radar. Its arrival was predicted and anticipated. People were alerted and thus had time to prepare. Most of the time, however, the storms of life are not so easily detected. They come without warning. Some storms are related to our family; some might hit our finances. The storms of life can be physical or emotional. The telephone rings, and suddenly a storm begins. A doctor walks into the room with a medical report—and without warning, a storm rages. An email in your inbox can set off a mighty storm. In the Sermon on the Mount, Jesus was alerting us: "If you will hear this sermon and do what it says, you will be ready for all the storms of life." That is an amazing deal.

After teaching all of the truths in this sermon, Jesus expressed these phenomenal words:

> Therefore everyone who hears these words of Mine and acts on them, may be compared to a wise man who built his house on the rock. And the rain fell, and the floods came, and the winds blew and slammed against that house; and yet it did not fall, for it had been founded on the rock. (Matthew 7:24-25)

My friends, *Jesus said the storms of life do not have to destroy us.* That's the purpose of the Sermon on the Mount. Jesus prepared His disciples for any storm that would come as they followed Him and served Him. The blessed life is the life that is covered and held firm by the strong, guiding hand of the blessed God. That is a deal!

Knowing this wonderful truth causes me to want to read, study, understand, and act on the Sermon on the Mount. Let's get started. No doubt, storms are coming. We can all be ready.

Living It Out

1. How does it change you to know that you can go through life with the hand of Sovereign God guiding and strengthening you?

    That, my friend, is the blessed life.

2. We are all building our lives on something. On what foundation are you building yours? Do you have a rock-solid foundation because of your faith in Jesus Christ, or is your foundation unstable, built on shifting sand?

    Jesus wants you to be prepared for any storm or blessing that comes your way. The Sermon on the Mount was written for you.

Let's Pray

> *Father, I recognize that storms will come my way. Please give me the wisdom I need to learn the lessons Jesus taught in the Sermon on the Mount so that I will be prepared for whatever comes into my life. Thank you for hearing and answering. I ask these things in the name of Jesus Christ. Amen.*

2

The Beatitudes: Path to Contentment, Part 1

Matthew 5:1-6

"He opened His mouth and began to teach them, saying . . ."
—Matthew 5:2

In the days before He delivered the Sermon on the Mount, Jesus had been extremely busy. As Matthew recorded, "Jesus was going throughout all Galilee, teaching in their synagogues and proclaiming the gospel of the kingdom, and healing every kind of disease and every kind of sickness among the people" (4:23). Great crowds followed as Jesus healed the sick and afflicted. Then we're told in Matthew 5:1 that Jesus "sat down." With His first few disciples gathered around Him, Jesus began to train them for ministry—and for the storms that would soon come their way.

Simon Peter was one of those men. The day would come when he would need to remember all that Jesus had taught. John was also one listening to Jesus that day. He too would one day need to recall the eternal truths he had received from the Master. And James (the brother of John) must have listened intently to the words that would eventually carry him with calm contentment through his greatest storm.

My friend, I pray we too attend carefully to Jesus as He showed us the path to contentment.

Inward Contentment

When Jesus said something more than once, He wanted us to understand exactly what He was saying. Because He used the word *blessed* nine times in the Beatitudes (Matthew 5:3-12), our Lord must have had something extremely important on His mind.

When researching the Greek word *blessed*, I noticed that some scholars say that blessed can be translated "happy." I don't know about you, but happy doesn't seem to meet my spiritual need in times of distress: happy are the poor, happy are the mourners, happy are those who are persecuted. Then I came across *The MacArthur New Testament Commentary*, which says blessed does indeed means happy, fortunate, or well off (1985, 142). Evidently, the ancient Greek poet Homer used the word to speak of a wealthy man, and Plato used the word to emphasize that those successful in business are blessed. But then MacArthur clarified the depth of the word blessed that Jesus used in Matthew 5: "The fullest meaning of the term, therefore, had to do with an *inward contentedness that is not affected by circumstances*" (1985, 141-42; emphasis added). Read this definition of blessed again: "Inward contentedness that is not affected by circumstances." Now that sounds like something I want! To be happy is good, but I'd rather learn to be inwardly content—whether in good times or in hard times. The apostles Peter, John, and James started their lives with Jesus by hanging on His every word. Through those utterly profound and never-before-heard-of truths, they gained the mettle and inner contentment to walk through their times of tribulation and persecution. How do we know?

+ Acts 12:6 reports that Peter slept, even though he was in prison, chained between two Roman soldiers and awaiting a death sentence from King Herod.

+ John, banished to the isle of Patmos because of his bold witness of Jesus Christ, sat alone on the Lord's day—singing and worshiping God (Revelation 1:9-10).

+ James, the first apostle to be martyred, beheaded by Herod Agrippa I, is remembered, along with other heroes of faith, as "one of whom the world was not worthy" (Acts 12:2, Hebrews 11:37-38).

Does inner contentment sound like something you need? If so, let's uncover what those apostles learned from Jesus that prepared them for whatever storms came their way.

Inner Experiences on the Path to Contentment

The Beatitudes interconnect. There is an indication that the first half of the Beatitudes—dealing with our inner experiences—leads to the second half—the outer evidence of our inner experiences. And taken together, they show us the clear path to spiritual satisfaction and inner contentment in any circumstance. Let's take our first step together, as we reflect on the inner experience of spiritual poverty.

The Inner Experience of

Spiritual poverty

Matthew 5:3

The poor in spirit — broken and repentant over sin — inherit the kingdom of heaven for eternity

> Blessed are the poor in spirit, for theirs is the kingdom of heaven.
> (Matthew 5:3)

This is an amazing passage of Scripture. As I understand it, the language of verse 3 says, "Blessed are the poor in spirit, for theirs, and only theirs, is the kingdom of heaven." In other words, the kingdom of heaven belongs only to those who have become poor in spirit. What does it mean to be "poor in spirit"? In Matthew 5:3, *poor* means "to cringe or to cower" (Vine 1940, 192) and is used to describe a beggar. This use of poor is uniquely different from the word Jesus used in Mark 12:42 to describe the "poor" widow who gave "all she owned," two small coins, to the temple treasury—the "poor" widow at least had something to give. Poor, as used in Matthew 5, relates to people so poor they have nothing to give; in fact, their depth of spiritual poverty is so deep, it's even shameful and embarrassing to them. These "poor" beggars cower in a dark corner, reaching out their hand to receive something, even as the other hand covers their face in shame. The word *spirit* in this verse has to do with our attitude. *The Complete Word Study New Testament* says spirit can mean "mental disposition" (Zodhiates 1991, 58). So, what was Jesus teaching?

Entrance to God's eternal kingdom is gained only when we have an attitude or mental disposition of spiritual poverty. We must see our soul's desperate need for a Savior. It's as if we reach out to Jesus with one hand, and cover our face with the other. I see a broken and repentant person saying, "Jesus, I'm so ashamed of my sin. I know that I do not deserve salvation—I'm spiritually nothing more than a beggar. But I need what you have to offer, so I'm reaching out to You. Will you give me the kingdom of heaven? Please, save me!" At that moment, our merciful Savior says, "I will do just that. You're the one I am looking for. Come into My kingdom."

What about you, are you poor in spirit? Have you experienced spiritual poverty? If you recognize that you are spiritually bankrupt and in need of the salvation Jesus offers, extend your hand and ask Him to be your Savior. He, in turn, will welcome you into His eternal kingdom. My friend, this is salvation, and the first step toward inner contentment in spite of any circumstance or storm.

The Inner Experience of

Mourning sin

Matthew 5:4

The poor in spirit, mournful over sin, are comforted by God's Spirit with forgiveness

Blessed are those who mourn, for they shall be comforted. (Matthew 5:4)

When we realize how great our need is for the salvation Jesus offers and how grievous our sin, we will mourn, even as we would mourn a death. *Comfort* can be translated "to call to one's side, or to be called near." What a beautiful illustration! In our disposition of humility, the indwelling Holy

Spirit, our Comforter, calls us near and comforts us with His forgiveness. Listen to His promise of forgiveness given in 1 John 1:9: "If we confess our sins, He is faithful and righteous to forgive us our sins and to cleanse us from all unrighteousness." Hallelujah, what a Savior!

Let me make an important point here. When we become poor in spirit and acknowledge our need for Christ, we become His children—but we do not become perfect. From time to time, sin will raise its ugly head. In fact, as Christians, we grow *more aware* of the presence of sin in our lives. Why? Because we now "have the mind of Christ" (1 Corinthians 2:16), and to continue on the path toward contentment and spiritual satisfaction, we must maintain an awareness of sin. When we see it, as ones who are poor in spirit, we must mourn that sin; we must deal with it.

Once we've become poor in spirit and mourned our sin, once we are comforted and forgiven by God, we are ready to take the next step toward spiritual satisfaction—gentle surrender to God.

The Inner Experience of

Gentle submission to God

Matthew 5:5

Broken, comforted, and forgiven, the made-gentle ones
willingly entrust their lives to the Master's control,
from whom they inherit all they need

Blessed are the gentle, for they shall inherit the earth. (Matthew 5:5)

According to *The MacArthur New Testament Commentary*, the word *gentle* carries the idea of a soft breeze (1985, 170); but it's also used to describe a wild horse that has been captured, bridled, and brought under control. Consider this. A wild, unbroken horse is uncontrollable. As an untamed, free animal, it roams wherever it pleases. There are no fences in the life of this animal; and there is nothing to direct its way. But one day, a cowboy throws a rope around the horse's neck, the cowboy tightens the rope, and the horse is stopped in its tracks. The cowboy places a bit and bridle in the mouth of this great animal, and soon the horse is under the guiding control of the one who holds the reins—the rider of the horse is now its master. The rider can lead the horse in any direction and make good use of its power and potential. What had been a wild, directionless, out-of-control animal is now made gentle.

Let's understand the parallel. When we become poor in spirit, we will mourn over our sin. Then, in broken repentance, we are brought under the control of the Lord and made gentle. We could say that we surrender all we are and all we have to the control of the Lord, for His use and glory.

Now look at what happens to those who have been mastered by the Master. Jesus told us that when we are under His control, we receive an inheritance: "Blessed are the gentle, for they shall inherit the earth" (Matthew 5:5). Those words seem strange to us, but they were not strange to the Jews of Jesus' day. In their minds, the Messiah would come to give the earth to the Jews, thereby meeting their every need. They would inherit the ultimate "land of milk and honey," which was the description of Canaan, the Promised Land. Jesus was teaching His Jewish disciples the benefit of trusting the Master: all of their needs would be met—including the needs that come as the result of a storm in life.

How does this work in our lives? When we become poor in spirit—humbly broken and repentant over our sin—we inherit the kingdom of God for eternity. Mournful over sin, we are comforted by God's Spirit with forgiveness. Made gentle by His forgiveness, we willingly entrust our lives to the Master's control. Why would we willingly surrender control of our lives to God? Because submitted to God our Provider, we see Him faithfully meet our needs, and His faithfulness causes us, with grateful hearts, to trust Him.

Now, while it's true that being submitted to Jesus allows Him to meet our needs, it's also true that He sometimes meets our needs in unexpected ways or in ways we don't understand (or like). We cannot expect Jesus to do things the way we would, for He sees what we don't and knows what we cannot. We can, however, expect that His ways are perfect and that He will always glorify the Father in what He does. Sometimes our highest response is just to say, "I know who You are and that You are good. So, even though I don't understand Your answer, I trust You in it." That, my friend, is the essence of faith.

The Inner Experience of

Hungering and thirsting for righteousness

Matthew 5:6

The forgiven and made-gentle ones, their needs met by God,
hunger and thirst for righteousness; they are fully satisfied by God,
to want only more of Him

Blessed are those who hunger and thirst for righteousness, for they shall be satisfied. (Matthew 5:6)

Once we experience the goodness of the Lord's forgiveness, comfort, and provision, we will naturally hunger and thirst for more of Him. Only a few times in my life have I seriously craved water, but I've never craved water without having some readily available to me. If we crave water, only water will meet that craving. We can down all of the soft drinks in the refrigerator, but our physical thirst will not be quenched; we must have water. When we crave righteousness, nothing else will do. Only righteousness will satisfy that craving. As in the following examples, it's possible to be so filled with God, so satisfied by Him, that we want only more of Him:

+ He satisfies us spiritually as we read His Word, yet we want to discover more of Him, verse by verse.

+ He satisfies us as we commune with Him in prayer, yet we long for the next intimate moment with our Lord.

+ He satisfies us as we fellowship with His bride, the church, and we eagerly contribute to her health and maturity.

+ He satisfies us by His faithfulness, so we trust Him even in life's difficulties.

+ He satisfies us by His forgiveness, so we desire to stay pure in thought and deed.

"They shall be satisfied" is not a one-time event. We're not satisfied once, and then it's finished. No, it's a perpetual satisfaction as we maintain an awareness of sin and the need to mourn it, as we maintain an attitude of trust in God's character and ways, and as we maintain our appetite for righteousness and for more of God.

Once again, notice this critical point. None of these inner experiences makes us perfect. Obviously, if we deeply desire righteousness, then more righteousness will be in our lives. But we should not expect perfection to come; that's not going to happen. Our dear Lord responds not to our perfection, but to our appetite for more of Him. When we desire righteousness even as a starving, thirsting person on the edge of death longs for food and water, then we will be satisfied—to want only more of Him.

Content At Last

Understanding the strength gained from these inner experiences almost causes me to say, "Well, come on storm! I'm living the blessed life, and I'm ready for anything you can throw at me." Note that I said *almost*. If you've ever been through a storm in life, you are not a volunteer for the next one. But my friend, it is coming, and you can be prepared.

The first few verses of the Beatitudes, Matthew 5:3-6, deal with our inner life. These inner experiences lead us straight to spiritual satisfaction and contentment in any circumstance. When we know the Lord will provide every need, we can be content in any storm. As we continue to hear and obey His Word, let's reflect on the outer evidences of our inner experiences.

Living It Out

1. When John MacArthur described the word *blessed*, he gave several meanings, including happy, fortunate, and well off. Then, he clarified Jesus' use of the word by saying, "The fullest meaning of the term had to do with an _____ _____ that is not affected by circumstances."

   Does that sound like something you want and need?

2. What does it mean to be spiritually bankrupt?

   Have you experienced this in your life? Briefly describe when and how this happened.

3. Have you been made gentle by the Master's touch?

   Do you listen for His voice and desire to please Him, or are you still like a wild horse—having an unbridled mind and tongue, and a temperament that seeks your own way in life?

   Any heart given to Jesus can be "made gentle."

4. Do you crave righteousness, even as a thirsty, dying man craves a drink of water? If so, you will be satisfied.

Let's Pray

Dear Jesus, just as the poor widow willingly gave all she possessed, two small coins, I too willingly give to You all that I am. Thank you that while I was still a sinner, you rescued me. Thank you for being my God and for leading me on a path to contentment. I ask these things in the name of Jesus Christ. Amen.

3

The Beatitudes:
Path to Contentment, Part 2

Matthew 5:7-12

"Rejoice and be glad, for your reward in heaven is great."
—Matthew 5:12

L ife is full of the evidence of our experiences. I have a scar on my
right knee. It is the outer evidence of surgery that took place when
I was a teenager. In fact, this scar is visible proof that something happened
inside my body.

As we learned in chapter 2, the Beatitudes interconnect. The first
half—dealing with our inner experiences—leads to the second half—the
outer evidence of our inner experiences. And taken together, the Beatitudes
show us the clear path to the blessed life: spiritual satisfaction and inner
contentment in any circumstance. Let's take our next step, as we continue
on our path to contentment.

Outer Evidences

In Matthew 5:7-12, we find at least four outer evidences, each connected
to an inner experience in the first verses of the Beatitudes.

+ *Mercy* (v. 7) describes the outer evidence of spiritual poverty (v. 3).

+ *Purity* (v. 8) describes the outer evidence of mourning our sin (v. 4).

+ *Peacemaking* (v. 9) describes the outer evidence of gentleness (v. 5).

+ *Persecution* (vv. 10-12) describes the outer evidence of hungering and thirsting for righteousness (v. 6).

Beginning with Matthew 5:7, let's see how this connection works, practically, in our lives.

The Inner Experience of	The Outer Evidence of Spiritual Poverty
Spiritual poverty	*Mercy*
Matthew 5:3	Matthew 5:7
The poor in spirit – broken and repentant over sin – inherit the kingdom of heaven	The poor in spirit received mercy, they in turn show mercy to others

Blessed are the merciful, for they shall receive mercy. (5:7)

In verse 7, Jesus said that blessed people—those in a state of contented living in spite of any circumstance—can be identified by the mercy they show others. Mercy flows naturally from the poor in spirit. Having recognized their spiritual poverty, these undeserving beggars reached out to receive the merciful forgiveness of our Savior; in turn, they can do no less for others. According to *The Expository Dictionary of New Testament Words, mercy* is "an outward manifestation of pity" (Vine 1940, 60); that is, mercy is not just a feeling of pity—it is an action. Merciful people are people of action. They see a need in the life of another and realize they can meet that need.

My wife, Jerri, is a merciful person. When she sees a need in someone's life, she cannot rest until that need is met. Presently, my mother lives in a nursing home in a town nearby. During our weekly visits with Mom, Jerri sees my mother's needs as well as the needs of others in that home, whether that need be a simple drink of water or a straightened blanket. Being the merciful person she is, Jerri has to act to help comfort those individuals. Merciful people not only see how they can assist someone but they also provide that assistance in some way.

When we receive God's goodness and grace toward us, we will naturally express mercy to others. That's why a Christian home can function different from a home without Christ. For example, a Christian dad received God's mercy; so, full of mercy himself, he shows mercy to his family. He sees their needs, and he desires to meet those needs. He loves, gives, and is compassionate. In turn, he can expect to receive the same from others. A Christian mom is kind, loving, and understanding; yet, she also has expectations of righteousness in her children, her marriage, and her own life. Christian children can respond to merciful parents with love, obedience, and kindness. God gives mercy, we show mercy, and we receive mercy from others. This sounds to me like the biblical principle of sowing and reaping: "He who sows sparingly will also reap sparingly, and he who sows bountifully will also reap bountifully" (2 Corinthians 9:6). In this way, mercy becomes perpetual, a lifestyle—and it never runs out.

In our study, we must grasp this important point: *It is God who does all these things in and through His people.* God is the initiator, the actor, the giver of inner experiences, and God is the source of all outer evidences. It is God who welcomes the poor in spirit into His kingdom. It is the God of mercy who comes near when we mourn over sin. God removes our sin and makes us gentle. God is the one who meets our needs as we submit our lives to His care. God Himself satisfies us when we hunger and thirst for righteousness, and it is God who fills His people with mercy. Let's not miss this fact, lest we attempt to produce in our lives (and take credit for) the things only God can bring about.

To apply this Beatitude to all of life, we could say, "Contented, in spite of circumstances, are those who express mercy. For when they give mercy, they will receive mercy." There is no doubt; mercy is the outer evidence of the inner experience of those who are poor in spirit.

The Inner Experience of	The Outer Evidence of Mourning Sin
Mourning sin	*Desire for purity*
Matthew 5:4	Matthew 5:8
The poor in spirit, mournful over sin, are comforted by God's Spirit with forgiveness	The poor in spirit, mournful of sin and comforted by God, desire purity and see God daily

Blessed are the pure in heart, for they shall see God. (5:8)

We read in Matthew 5:8 of another outer evidence of spiritual poverty. Notice how verse 4, "Blessed are those who mourn, for they shall be comforted," relates to verse 8, "Blessed are the pure in heart, for they shall see God." Purity is the outer evidence that we have become poor in spirit and have mourned over sin. When we mourn over sin, the last thing we want in our life is more sin. Instead, we desire to be pure in heart.

During the writing of this book, our nation was shocked with the evidence of adultery by yet another of our leading politicians—a man whom many, at one time, favored as a presidential candidate. His fall came when the facts were presented of his affair with a member of his staff; thereafter, his life and reputation crumbled. Today, he is known not as a respected politician who could have been president of the United States, but as a man shamed by his immorality, who threw away his reputation and his family, and who now faces a possible prison term for related charges. It is not my desire to further shame this individual; I pray for him and for his family, and I would gladly minister to him at any time. But here's the point. How different might his life have been (and still could be) had he become "poor in spirit" and mourned over his sin? When temptation to commit adultery came upon him, instead of falling to the temptation, the grateful desire of his heart would have been to live before God in purity. How different his life could still be.

While there are natural consequences of sin, we can be thankful that God's offer of salvation remains. That's good news. It's never too late to repent and receive God's forgiveness! It's never too late for a pure heart. Not for this fallen father and public figure, not for you, not for me.

"Blessed are the pure in heart." The Bible speaks of four types of purity: creative purity, positional purity, actual purity, and practical purity.

Creative purity is the state of earth and creation in the beginning. "God saw all that He had made, and behold, it was very good" (Genesis 1:31). Before sin, toil, pain, and death entered (Genesis 3), God looked on all He had created—light, earth, seas, vegetation, the sun, the moon, stars, every living creature—and pronounced them pure and right and "very good."

Positional purity refers to a Christian's new life in Christ. This type of purity is important. My life is not always pure, even though I'm a Christian. There are things God wants to change in all of us, and I hope He's changing me daily as I attempt to walk with Him. But as a Christian, I am in Christ. That's my position. "I have been crucified with Christ; and it is no longer I who live, but Christ lives in me; and the life which I now live in the flesh I live by faith in the Son of God, who loved me and gave Himself up for me" (Galatians 2:20). So, when the Father looks at me, He sees Christ—that is, He sees purity. Positionally, therefore, I am pure.

Actual purity is not sin-filled earth, but heaven, where God will make "all things new" (Revelation 21:5). "And nothing unclean, and no one who practices abomination and lying, shall ever come into it, but only those whose names are written in the Lamb's book of life" (Revelation 21:27).

Practical purity is emphasized in the Sermon on the Mount. We can be thankful that purity is *not* perfection. Otherwise, we would have to walk through life with our head hanging, feeling lousy and fatalistically hopeless. No! Purity is the condition of those who have acknowledged their spiritual poverty. When God shows us an area of sin—no matter the sin, no matter how frequent—we mourn it, confess it, turn from it, and receive His forgiveness. We say with thankfulness and passion, "I'm forgiven! I'm changed—a new person in Christ. I can walk in God's comfort and peace." "Blessed are the pure in heart."

Notice the end of Matthew 5:8: "for [the pure in heart] shall see God." It is so important that we understand in what ways people of purity will see God. The Greek word used for *see* relates to intimately experiencing God every day. Perhaps this story will help illustrate experiencing, or seeing, someone.

Several years ago, my wife, Jerri, and I had the joy of taking a mission trip to Southeast Asia with our friends Tom and Jeannie Elliff. There was a portion of this trip, however, that made me especially nervous. I remember the day well because it was Mother's Day. After we had spent a few days training some wonderful believers in that country, Jerri and Jeannie were to lead a women's retreat, while Tom and I left our wives for three days to trek through the rain forest to an area unreached by the gospel.

Well, the time came for us to part ways. Tom and I crawled into the back of an old car as we watched our wives climb into the back of an old truck. (To this day, I don't understand why the male passenger in the cab did not get out and let the women ride inside the cab, but he didn't.) As our wives settled into the bed of the truck, Tom and I rode by, rolled down the windows, and called out to our wives, "Happy Mother's Day!" This is when I got nervous. I had no idea where Jerri was going. I had no address or phone number by which to reach her. We only knew they were supposed to be met by some women in some other town to lead a retreat somewhere. Even though Tom assured me everything would be all right, I was uncomfortable not being able to have contact with my wife.

During the days apart from our wives, Tom and I had the opportunity to share the gospel and pray with people who were truly unreached by the gospel. Those were indeed an amazing few days. Nonetheless, I longed to *see* Jerri. The day finally came when we made our trip to a small town and a café where Jerri and Jeannie were to meet us. As I climbed out of the car, I heard a most wonderful voice. It was Jerri's voice, and she simply said, "Ted, I'm up here." I looked up to the rooftop of that little café and saw the most beautiful creature in the world. There was Jerri, waiting for me. In that glorious moment, I heard her voice. I saw her face. I could not get to her fast enough. I was seeing my wife. I was experiencing her.

Do you see the truth? Just as I saw and experienced my wife that day, the pure in heart will see and experience God—every day they live. In our deep longing for purity and for God, He responds. How do we see God? Through any temptation or storm, we can maintain purity—because we experience His presence and His strength. In His presence, we gain His wisdom. In times of trouble, He is available to us. Whether young or old, a businessperson or a student, our status in life does not matter. God responds to *purity* with His presence. We could say this truth in many ways.

✦ "Blessed are those who are disciplined in their walk with God, for they will walk with Him daily."

✦ "Blessed are those who seek to be pure in heart, for they will see God in every circumstance."

✦ "Blessed are those who abide in His Word and live obediently, for they will experience all He has to give them."

✦ "Blessed are these, because they experience God today, in whatever circumstance they need Him."

✦ David said it this way: "He who does these things will never be shaken" (Psalm 15:5).

What have we seen so far concerning this outer evidence of our inner experience? We have seen that purity in our lives is the evidence of mourning over sin. God responds to purity, and we will experience Him in all our ways.

The Inner Experience of *Gentle submission to God* Matthew 5:5	The Outer Evidence of Gentle Submission to God *Seeking peace in others* Matthew 5:9
Broken, comforted, and forgiven, the made-gentle ones willingly entrust their lives to the Master's control, from whom they inherit all they need	Pure in heart, gentle, and submitted to the Master's control, the sons of God seek God's highest good for others

Blessed are the peacemakers, for they shall be called sons of God. (5:9)

We normally think of a peacemaker as one who reconciles adversaries, perhaps even one who "calms the waters." These are certainly good actions for us to undertake, but that meaning doesn't seem to apply to Matthew 5:9.

Remember from chapter 2 the analogy of a wild horse? Before being broken and bridled, that creature is powerful but aimless, strong but uncontrollable. After the work of the cowboy, however, that same horse—with all its power, stamina, and potential—is made gentle and useful to the one who holds the reins. The same is true for us. When mastered by the Master, we too are made gentle and useful, our lives willingly placed under the blessed control of the Lord Jesus. From Matthew 5:9, we learn that peacemaking is the natural evidence flowing from the Christ-follower who has been made gentle.

The word *peacemaker* is constructed from two words. *Maker* obviously means "one who makes or produces something." *Peace* in this verse concerns the welfare of others. Daily submitted to God, a maker of peace becomes a useful channel (think horse) of God's grace by actively fostering God's best in others. For example, when love or forgiveness is needed, the peacemaker is one God can work through to bring love and forgiveness. Whether in the workplace or in the church, a peacemaker says, "Above all else, I want God's good for those around me." In a family, a peacemaker says, "It's my responsibility to make sure everyone in my family has the opportunity to experience God's best." Made-gentle ones seek to produce God's best in others. By the way, peacemaking isn't for believers wanting to loiter on the edge of a Christian walk. It's not a lifestyle for the faint-hearted. Peacemaking is for those ready to surrender their power, stamina, and potential to the Master's skillful hand.

The apostle Paul, in Philippians 2:1-5, described *how* we seek God's highest good for those around us.

> Therefore if there is any encouragement in Christ, if there is any consolation of love, if there is any fellowship of the Spirit, if any affection and compassion, . . . (v. 1)

Using the apostle Paul's exhortation, we can ask ourselves a series of questions that, taken together, identify the lifestyle of a peacemaker.

+ Is there any encouragement in Christ? Are others encouraged when they meet us, because we are Christians?

+ Is there any consolation of love? Are others consoled by the love we show because we are Christians?

+ Is there any fellowship of the Spirit? Do other people experience the Spirit of God when they spend time with you or me? Because the Spirit of God lives in every believer, shouldn't it be natural for others to experience Him when they experience a Christian?

✦   Is there any affection and compassion? As we interact with our family, in the marketplace, and in our workplace, do people experience the affection and compassion of Christ in our words and actions?

Paul must have assumed he would hear a resounding yes to each of these questions. He then continued, by challenging us to embrace one primary goal, to be "intent on one purpose":

Make my joy complete by being of the same mind, maintaining the same love, united in spirit, intent on one purpose. Do nothing from selfishness or empty conceit, but with humility of mind regard one another as more important than yourselves; do not merely look out for your own personal interests, but also for the interests of others. Have this attitude in yourselves which was also in Christ Jesus. (Philippians 2:2-5)

The one purpose that drives the actions of a peacemaker, that guides all interactions with family, coworkers, and fellow believers, is to "do nothing from selfishness or empty conceit but with humility of mind regard one another as more important than yourselves." Now I ask, is there any word or action that "nothing" fails to cover? No. "Nothing" means nothing! It seems to me that Paul has challenged all areas of our lives in these verses.

What might Paul's challenge look like practically if we applied it, say, tomorrow morning? A husband would take his wife's hand at the breakfast table and say, "Sweetheart, from this day forward, your interests are more important than mine." Children would say to their parents, "Mom, Dad, today is a new day. My greatest concern will be to honor God and you with my life." Imagine a Christian businessperson saying to his or her employees, "I have good news. As of today, this business will protect and promote your interests, not just the bottom line." Members of a congregation would commit to one another: "From now on, we will seek God's kingdom first, not our own interests. We will decrease, so He can increase." I'm telling you revival would break out if the church committed to obey the Word of God and to seek the highest good of others.

Now let's listen to and learn from the Master as we look at the final words of Matthew 5:9: "For [peacemakers] shall be *called* sons of God" (emphasis added). The word *called* has to do with your surname, the name that identifies the family to which you belong. Do you see what Jesus was teaching? The character quality that identifies us as members of the family of God is peacemaking.

I graduated from high school in Miami, Oklahoma, where my father worked as the administrator of the local hospital. As a businessman and a minister, Dad always wore a suit to work, which caused him to be a customer of Tom Barton, owner of the men's clothing store. Some years after my parents had moved away from Miami, my wife and I returned to see her parents. One day, simply needing a place to go while Jerri shopped, I walked into Mr. Barton's store. I looked around a little and then started toward the door. From the back of the store, Mr. Barton called out, "You *have* to be related to Bill Kersh. Are you Ted?" I responded that I was indeed Ted Kersh. Out of curiosity, I asked, "Mr. Barton, how in the world did you know I was the son of Bill Kersh? You were behind me, at the back of the store. How did you know who I was?" Mr. Barton said, "Well, Ted, you walk just like your father."

Tom Barton identified me by the way I walk. This is what Jesus was saying when He declared, "They shall be called sons of God." A child of God can be recognized by the way he or she walks. When we live a Philippians 2 lifestyle, as peacemakers who put the interests of others first, we can be identified as God's children. We will remind others of Jesus. How's your walk these days? Determine to wake up tomorrow morning intent on seeking God's highest good for others, on putting the interests of others first. Blessed are peacemakers, because their surname will be "sons of God."

The Inner Experience of	The Outer Evidence of
Hungering and thirsting for righteousness	Hungering and Thirsting for Righteousness
	Persecution
Matthew 5:6	Matthew 5:10
The forgiven and made-gentle ones, their needs met by God, hunger and thirst for righteousness; they are fully satisfied by God, to want only more of Him	Those fully satisfied by God alone, who hunger and thirst for more of Him, will be persecuted on earth but rewarded greatly in heaven

> Blessed are those who have been persecuted for the sake of righteousness, for theirs is the kingdom of God. (5:10)

We must examine one final, less-than-comfortable evidence of spiritual poverty. Here too we'll discover that following Christ is not for the faint of heart. In this case, skipping past verses 10-12 would be easier, but we can't. Jesus could have ended the Beatitudes by saying, "Just live a godly life and you will prosper. Live in faith and you'll be healthy, wealthy, and wise," but He didn't. To face Jesus' words in verse 10 is not only to face the truth but also to be prepared, aware, and strong when we are persecuted for following Christ.

Remember, verse 10 describes the result of practicing verse 6. Jesus taught in this beatitude that those who hunger and thirst after righteousness will be persecuted. This is a promise from the Word of God. If we desire to live godly lives in this ungodly world, then we will experience persecution. Jesus then expounded on the persecution Christ-followers can expect:

> Blessed are you when people insult you and persecute you, and falsely say all kinds of evil against you because of Me. Rejoice and be glad, for your reward in heaven is great; for in the same way they persecuted the prophets who were before you. (Matthew 5:11-12)

Insults can be verbal, in-your-face, disrespectful criticisms or rude, abusive remarks. Persecution can be physical mistreatment, abuse, or discrimination.

Speaking evil can be behind-your-back, disparaging, defaming, or slanderous remarks. But did you notice that Jesus called the receivers of persecution "blessed"? Even more, He commanded, "Rejoice and be glad." I don't know about you, but I'm not there yet. While persecution hasn't been my experience, jumping for joy is not what I imagine that my response would be. Why would Jesus command us to rejoice and be glad? Because the prophets of God were persecuted—David, Hosea, Daniel, Jeremiah, Isaiah, Ezekiel—so we would be in good company! Persecution is simply a reminder that we are part of God's kingdom, that because we long for more of God, our great reward awaits us in His eternal kingdom. This earth is neither our home nor our reward.

Remember what the apostle Paul said to Timothy, even as Paul neared his own execution? "Indeed, all who desire to live godly in Christ Jesus will be persecuted" (2 Timothy 3:12). Paul was saying to Timothy and to us, "Sure there are challenges for Christ's followers. But don't choose to coast through your Christian life. Dig in deep. We go through all these things not alone, but with our strong Savior. To gain Christ and the eternal reward is well worth it." Soon after writing those words, Paul himself triumphantly entered eternity to gain his reward. Christian tradition says he was beheaded.

After Jesus announced to His disciples the costs associated with being a Christ-follower, He ended the Beatitudes this way: "You are the salt of the earth; but if the salt has become tasteless, how can it be made salty *again*? It is no longer good for anything, except to be thrown out and trampled under foot by men" (Matthew 5:13). As we know, Jesus was preparing His disciples then—and every disciple to follow—to stand firm and content through all of life's troubles, including persecution. Jesus knew the eternal outcome, and He wanted His own to reach that reward. In addition, He knew that living as salt and light was a big deal—the world's eternal destiny was at stake.

I've been called to jury duty only a couple of times. In my first experience, I was dismissed when they learned I was a pastor. Nevertheless, I remember an attorney's charge to those of us in the room: "Whatever you do, listen to the evidence. Just follow the evidence." Let's examine the evidence of our lives. Do others see that we're poor in spirit because we show mercy, or that we're pure in heart because we turn from sin, or under the control of the living God because we are gentle? Is there evidence that we hunger and thirst for God because we seek His highest for those around us? Do others see that we're poor in spirit?

Why have we taken a lot of time to talk about the experience of being poor in spirit and the outer evidences that result? Because this is what leads to the blessed life. This is the beginning of the life prepared for any storm. Now we're ready to listen to our Lord teach the rest of the Sermon on the Mount. Get ready for an exciting journey as we approach the blessed life.

Living It Out

1. Do you have the joy of experiencing God every day, of intimately walking with Him in good times and bad?

   Are you learning from Him?

   These blessings are reserved for the pure in heart. God eagerly desires to reveal Himself to *you*.

2. According to 2 Timothy 3:12, "All who desire to live godly in Christ Jesus will be _____."

   Are you ready to stand for Christ come what may?

✦ ✦ ✦

Let's Pray

> *Father, You are concerned about the condition of my heart and so am I. Please make me ready to stand for You every moment of every day. I ask these things in the name of Jesus Christ. Amen.*

4

Christian Living:
Is It Really a Big Deal?

Matthew 5:13-16

"You are the salt of the earth. You are the light of the world."
—Matthew 5:13, 14

Some things in life really are a "big deal," and some experiences in life that we think are important really are not very important at all. As much as I hate to admit it, it's really not very important who wins the national championship in college football. I may lose a few readers with that statement, but come on. Do you know who won the national championship last year? A few from the winning school (and certainly from the losing school) might know, but for most of us, who won that game mattered for only about thirty seconds. It's not a *big* deal.

Then again, some things in life really are a big deal. Like side-view mirrors on your car. When she was sixteen, our daughter, Rebekah (Bekah to most of us), had a great little car. (I loved that '95 Camaro. In fact, I helped her buy it because I could see myself driving it. Dads are like that you know.) I remember the day Bekah came through the house carrying one of the side-view mirrors. "Dad, as I was pulling my car in the garage, I hit the middle post of the garage doors, and I knocked this mirror off the passenger side. But don't worry about it, Dad, I don't use this one anyway.

It's not a big deal." I remember saying something like, "Not a big deal? Do you not ever move from the left lane to the right lane?"

Now, I must quickly say that my daughter is a wonderful driver today. But here's the lesson. Whether we realize it or not, some things in life really are big deals, and one of the biggest is living the Christian life. We've just spent a good deal of time studying the Beatitudes, in which Jesus spent an amazing amount of energy teaching us to be poor in spirit. After teaching the Beatitudes, Jesus immediately began telling us about living the Christian life. You can call this life the Christian life or the life of a disciple. You can call it the Spirit-led life or whatever you want to call it. The fact is, living the Christian life is a "big deal." Remember that at the end of the Sermon on the Mount, Jesus offered us an amazing deal: If we will hear this sermon and do what it says, then we will be ready for all the storms of life.

> Therefore everyone who hears these words of Mine and acts on them, may be compared to a wise man who built his house on the rock. And the rain fell, and the floods came, and the winds blew and slammed against that house; and yet it did not fall, for it had been founded on the rock. (Matthew 7:24-25)

In the next verses and chapters of Matthew, Jesus taught us how to build our lives on the rock—He taught us how to live the Christian life. To be ready to handle the storms that will come our way, let's listen carefully and do all that Jesus instructed.

Salt and Light: The Church

Matthew 5:13-16 tells us why it is a big deal to live the Christian life.

> You are the salt of the earth; but if the salt has become tasteless, how can it be made salty *again*? It is no longer good for anything, except to be thrown out and trampled under foot by men.
>
> You are the light of the world. A city set on a hill cannot be hidden; nor does anyone light a lamp and put it under a basket,

but on the lampstand, and it gives light to all who are in the house.

Let your light shine before men in such a way that they may see your good works, and glorify your Father who is in heaven. (Matthew 5:13–16)

In verses 13–14, Jesus entrusted to His disciples two significant responsibilities: "You are the salt of the earth" and "You are the light of the world." In both verses, Jesus spoke the word *you* emphatically and with passion. In doing so, He emphasized that there is something distinctive about the lives of His followers. Something unique sets His disciples apart from everyone else. That distinctiveness has to do with Christians' responsibility in this world to live as salt and light. As I understand the language of these verses, Jesus was saying, "You and only you are the salt of the earth," and "You and only you are the light of the world."

You, in both verses, is not only emphatic but it is also plural. Jesus directly addressed the disciples assembled at His feet that day as well as every believer since. The plural word *you* tells me that I must have other believers if I'm to be the salt of the earth, and I must have other believers if I'm to be the light of the world. Whatever it means for me to be salt and light, I cannot do it by myself. I need you, and you need me. In addition, for the world to be influenced, the whole body of Christ, the church, must accept the responsibility and seriousness of righteous Christian living. The church is the salt and the light Jesus uses to influence and illuminate the world.

Although "you" in these verses is plural, the words "salt" and "light" are singular. Jesus was teaching us, "You are all *the salt* of the earth. You are all *the light* of the world." In other words, we're it; there are no others. Godly influence and the reflection of Christ will come to this world only from the body of Christ, the church. In the power of the Holy Spirit, no one else and nothing else can fulfill this charge. By the way, that charge is not optional. We can't opt out by saying any of the following:

+ "It's not my responsibility. Let the pastor do it."

+ "That's not for me, I'm too [fill in the blank]."

+ "No, I'm no good at [fill in the blank]. Maybe someone else will help."

+   "Someone else will have to, because I don't have enough
    [fill in the blank]."

+   "Isn't that what the church staff gets paid to do?"

If I, Ted Kersh, do not do whatever salt does in this earth, then whatever
salt does will not be done. If I do not do what light does, then whatever
is supposed to happen in reference to light will not happen. I have a
unique position in being salt and light every day. You do as well. Jesus was
emphatic!

The Functions of Salt

Jesus gave the charge, and it's ours to take up. So, if we the church were
to function as salt, what might that look like? What exactly does salt do?
Though I'm not a scientist, a brief study of salt reveals several of its values.

+   Salt stops decay and corruption. It preserves and saves
    whatever it touches. If you and I are the salt of the earth, we
    actively function as God's agents, present on earth, to stop
    decay and corruption.

+   Salt is a preservative. Yet, it operates as a preservative only
    when in direct contact with whatever needs to be preserved.
    Salt saves only as it touches. Even so, the church, God's agent
    of salt, can influence our world not by isolation, but by our
    direct and active touch.

+   Salt is an element essential for life. Without salt, people die.
    The church, as the activated substance of Christ on earth,
    imperatively proclaims salvation in Christ. As the apostle
    Paul proclaimed, "And there is salvation in no one else; for
    there is no other name under heaven that has been given
    among men, by which we must be saved" (Acts 4:12). Christ
    alone is essential for life.

+   Salt as a seasoning is unique in its flavor. As the church
    displays the properties and character of Christ, we dispense
    to the world the savor of Christ. Living the Christian life

is a big deal—because it makes others thirsty for more of Christ.

+ Salt is an ingredient with active healing and therapeutic properties. Need on earth is evident and vast. Just read the newspaper or notice the person working in the cubicle next to you. Whether for physical, emotional, or spiritual healing, you and I are Christ's agents to soothe and even bring healing to His creation.

How different might people and circumstances on earth be if you and I actively function, every moment, as the salt of Christ on earth? I can't wait to get started. How about you?

The Functions of Light

And what about light? Light shows people the way out of darkness. If we are the light of the world, then we have the unique responsibility (and honor) of leading people out of the darkness of sin and into the light of Jesus.

> You are the light of the world. A city set on a hill cannot be hidden; nor does anyone light a lamp and put it under a basket, but on the lampstand, and it gives light to all who are in the house. (Matthew 5:14-15)

Not long ago, I saw a photograph of the Korean peninsula. This image, taken by a U.S. defense satellite, displays the city lights of North and South Korea at night. As you look toward North Korea, the only light in the photograph is a small cluster visible around the home of the government's dictatorial leader. The rest of the country sits in darkness. If you look south of the Demilitarized Zone, however, the photograph explodes with light. The contrast is telling. South Korea is a free society. Because the people are free—personally, politically, economically, educationally, and spiritually—South Korea is a bright, thriving, well-lit nation. In contrast, all systems of North Korea are tightly controlled and severely restricted.

The nation, its economy, and its people are thus left in great darkness by a sinful, cruel kleptocrat. But what you need to know is that there is a light shining in South Korea that is greater than any city lights at night: the light of Christianity. South Koreans display not only physical light but they also reflect great spiritual light at home and around the world. What a picture of Christ's charge to the church! We are the light of the world. Our job is to show people how to escape darkness and sin through Jesus Christ. Christ's followers are to reflect to all within view the true Light of the world.

Functioning as salt and light in our world is the way Jesus described the Christian life. My Christ-following friend, do you see how important you are to Jesus? Without you and other believers, there is no light. Without you and other believers, there is no salt. The world in which we live tries to humanly solve humanity's problems, but the fact is that no political system, no government, no political leader can be salt and light in this world. No philosophy and no amount of education can add the salt and light our world needs. Neither money nor power can solve the problems of decay and darkness. *You and I* are the salt. *You and I* are the light. Righteous Christian living is a "really big deal." But that's not all.

The Danger of Dysfunction

What happens if Christians do not function in our world as salt? Remember Jesus' sober warning recorded in Matthew 5:13? "You are the salt of the earth; but if the salt has become tasteless, how can it be made salty again? It is no longer good for anything, except to be thrown out and trampled under foot by men." The word *good* can mean "force" or "ability." So, the verse could be paraphrased like this: "Once the salt has lost its flavor, it no longer has the force or the ability to influence what it touches." It's important to know that salt cannot lose its saltiness. It can, however, lose its savor, its strength. Salt can lose its ability to season and preserve. In short, when salt is diluted, it becomes of no effect. My friend, we cannot lose our salvation, but we can lose our flavor. It's possible to go through the motions of a Christian but no longer display the properties and character of Christ. If we allow ourselves to become diluted by the sin of the world, we lose our value of dispensing the savor of Christ. If we let the ways of the world mix with our lives, we lose our influence to stop decay and corruption. In other words, we become dysfunctional believers.

Every day, people on their way to hell walk right past dysfunctional Christians, and those dysfunctional Christians have not the strength or ability to touch their lives. Make no mistake. Living a Christian life really is a big deal. And yet, as difficult as it might be to face this truth, Christians losing their influence is not the greatest truth in this passage of Scripture.

To Glorify the Father: Our Highest Opportunity

Jesus gave the ultimate reason for living the Christian life. "Let your light shine before men in such a way that they may see your good works, and glorify your Father who is in heaven" (Matthew 5:16). My Christian friend, we have an amazing responsibility and opportunity to "glorify your Father who is in heaven." What does it mean to glorify God? The word *glorify* means "to make glorious and full of glory," "to honor," or "to magnify." In other words, we are to live in such a way that people see that our God is big in our life.

Recently, I heard my oldest son, Paul, say something that stuck in my mind. While speaking to a group of parents, my son said, "It seems to me that our responsibility is to raise our children in such a way that their lives brag on Jesus." I immediately thought, *That's it! That's exactly what it means to glorify the Father.* We have the responsibility to live a life that brags on Jesus.

When I started writing this chapter, I knew that living for Christ was a big deal. But after this study, I realize it's an even bigger deal than I imagined. As Christ-followers, you and I have a great responsibility. Before we go further, perhaps we should make a commitment. Let this be your prayer today:

Father, today I clearly hear the charge You gave Your followers. I now realize my responsibility to be salt and light in this world. I confess that there are times when my life has not stopped decay, when I have not lived as light that leads people to you. Father, I ask You to forgive me! I understand and accept my responsibility to influence the world in which I live.

I want to be useful to You. I commit to You today not to be one who is set aside. Everywhere I go, help me to influence others for You. With You as my strength, I will be salt and light in this world. Father, it's a big deal for me to live the Christian life! I ask these things in the name of Jesus. Amen!

Living It Out

1. Consider the spiritual truths concerning salt, its qualities, and its uses. Are any of those characteristics true of you?

   Which ones?

   Which do you want to possess?

2. Describe a current situation in which you need to live as salt and light.

3. On what things would people say that you brag—your position, wealth, possessions, abilities, children?

   How far down the bragging line would Jesus be?

4. To *glorify* God means "to make glorious and full of glory," "to honor," or "to magnify." Beginning tomorrow, in what ways can you "brag on Jesus" with your life?

Let's Pray
> *Father, I want to be salt and light to someone in this sin-sick world. Please help it to be obvious to others that I am a Christ-follower. I understand that it really is a big deal! I ask these things in the name of Jesus Christ. Amen.*

5

Salt and Light in Relationships

Matthew 5:17-26

Everyone who is angry with his brother shall be guilty before the court;
and whoever says to his brother, "You good-for-nothing," shall be guilty
before the supreme court; and whoever says, "You fool," shall be guilty
enough to go into the fiery hell.
—Matthew 5:22

Some things are almost impossible to describe. I remember the great preacher Dr. Adrian Rogers saying, "I do not know how to describe Spirit-filled preaching, but I sure know it when I hear it." If you've heard enough sermons, you understand exactly what Dr. Rogers was saying. How do you describe Spirit-filled preaching?

How do you describe love? I can't describe it, but I sure know that I'm in love with my wife. We met while in high school in Miami, Oklahoma. I had just moved to that small town in northeastern Oklahoma; Jerri had lived there all of her life. She was a Miami "Wardog" born and bred; I was a Wardog transplant. When Jerri and I started dating, love between us was immediate and strong. We would go to a movie and then to the local pizza parlor, where we had our own table, one close to the thermostat. If Jerri thought the room was chilly, being the considerate man that I am, I would adjust the heat. If she thought the room too hot, I made the room cooler.

Whether the other patrons were hot or cold mattered nothing to me. Only Jerri and her comfort mattered.

After taking Jerri home from a date, I would jump into my '66 blue Mustang (just wanted you to know I had one) and fly home. (Jerri and I lived on different sides of the tracks, and we still argue about who lived on the *wrong* side of those tracks.) I would drive the entire length of the city of Miami, seven very long miles, run into the house, grab the telephone, and call Jerri. When she answered the phone, my first words were, "Hey, what are you doing?" There was something wonderful about hearing her breathe those special words, "Oh, nothing. What are you doing?" Friends, that's love! I cannot describe it, but I know I still experience it today. After more than forty years of marriage, I still call her and say, "Hey, what are you doing?" And she still sweetly replies, "Oh, nothing. What are you doing?" I knew after our first date that I was going to marry Jerri, though I can't describe how I knew it. How do you describe love?

How do you describe salt and light? Jesus knew that for us to understand what it means to live as the salt of the earth and the light of the world, He would need to describe what that life would look like practically; so He began by addressing the origin of the salt-and-light life, the heart.

The Inward Application of the Law

During His three short years of ministry, Jesus not only declared the good news that the kingdom of God had come but He also described that kingdom in every way imaginable, trying to overcome a range of cultural and religious paradigms. For example, the typical Jewish expectation was that the Messiah would come as a political leader, run the cruel Romans out of the provinces, and set up a political kingdom with King Messiah on the throne. The only trouble is, that was not exactly God's plan, which is why Jesus worked so hard to describe a God-ordained kingdom and king, who would rule not from an earthbound throne, but from an internal throne—the heart.

Well, because the Old Testament systems were well established (the temple sacrifices, for instance), one important clarification Jesus had to make was His relationship to those systems. Would He declare null and void the Old Testament principles?

> Do not think that I came to abolish the Law or the Prophets; I
> did not come to abolish but to fulfill. For truly I say to you, until
> heaven and earth pass away, not the smallest letter or stroke shall
> pass from the Law until all is accomplished.
>
> Whoever then annuls one of the least of these
> commandments, and teaches others to do the same, shall be
> called least in the kingdom of heaven; but whoever keeps and
> teaches them, he shall be called great in the kingdom of heaven.
> (Matthew 5:17-19)

Imagine a child's coloring book (illustration by Henry 1961). On each page is an outline of a simple, recognizable object, but it is merely an outline. The outline is important, nonetheless, for it guides us in anticipating what is intended, what is to fully come, what is needed to complete the picture, though the outline isn't the complete picture. Similarly, the laws and principles set forth in the Ten Commandments (Exodus 20) were the external outline of God's law and kingdom, and they served a purpose for a time, that is, until God sent the real thing—Jesus. He came to live among us as the full, living-color completion of the outline. The external law was important, but Jesus embodied the law; He unfolded it before our eyes and moved it into our hearts. King Jesus established God's kingdom within our hearts.

To illustrate for us the life lived as salt and light, Jesus first described what that life is *not*, and for an illustration, He needed only to point to the scribes and Pharisees.

> For I say to you that unless your righteousness surpasses that
> of the scribes and Pharisees, you will not enter the kingdom of
> heaven. (Matthew 5:20)

The people of Jesus' day considered the scribes and Pharisees to be "righteous" folk. They worked hard to follow the ceremonial laws of the Old Testament, but their hearts were anything but godly. Unimpressed by the false piety of the scribes and Pharisees, Jesus told His followers that their righteousness must exceed that of the scribes and Pharisees because salt-and-light living is not outward piety, it is inward purity. God's law reaches further and deeper than mere displays of outward self-righteousness.

Righteous Living 101, Jesus indicated, begins in the deepest thoughts and activities of the heart. And with that, He exposed a problem common to most of us—anger.

The Destruction of Anger

Many years ago, while serving on the staff of First Baptist Church, McAlester, Oklahoma, I had an experience that taught me the seriousness of anger. McAlester is home to the Oklahoma State Penitentiary, built as a maximum-security facility in 1908 by the labor of incarcerated felons brought in from a Kansas prison. One of my staff responsibilities (and privileges) was to preach each week at the "state pen." Every Saturday evening, I made my way through security to preach to a large group of inmates. I developed some good relationships during those meetings; one in particular was with a man (we'll call him Pete) who looked like any man you might know. Pete was a nice-looking, intelligent, well-spoken man. In fact, had I not known the truth about him, I would have thought he was actually innocent and had been wrongly convicted. But one day he told me the facts.

Pete and his wife lived in another state and had been married for several years. For some reason, he had grown suspicious of her faithfulness to him, so he started following her. Eventually, he confirmed his worst fears—his wife was indeed involved with another man. At this point, with anger boiling in his heart and mind, Pete made a plan to track the man down.

Upon discovering that his wife's lover lived in Oklahoma, my friend headed straight to the state, a drive that took several hours. His original plan was just to confront the man and, at the most, beat him up. But the farther he drove, mile by mile, his seething anger exploded into an uncontrollable rage. Pete eventually arrived in Oklahoma, and when he found the man, my clean-cut businessman friend did not stop with beating his wife's lover—Pete killed the man. My friend was soon apprehended, tried, and sentenced to life in prison.

After Pete finished telling his story, I confessed to him that I could hardly believe *he* had committed murder. Then my friend declared a tragically learned truth, one that still haunts me today. He said, "Ted, never be surprised at what anger can do. Anger will take you where you never intended to go."

Knowing the destruction of anger, Jesus ratcheted up the discussion and the consequences of anger.

> You have heard that the ancients were told, "You shall not commit murder" and "Whoever commits murder shall be liable to the court."
>
> But I say to you that everyone who is angry with his brother shall be guilty before the court. (Matthew 5:21-22)

Does it seem odd to you that Jesus would begin His teaching on anger with thoughts concerning murder? I mean, after all, aren't we just talking about a little irritability in the life of a Christian? How did we jump from anger to murder?

It's critical that we understand the historical context of Jesus' teaching. The "ancients" to whom Jesus referred were the Old Testament rabbis and scribes. They knew God's sixth commandment by heart—"You shall not commit murder"—and they knew that, according to civil law, committing the physical act of murder would land you squarely before a courtroom judge. As was true for the other nine commandments, murder was as serious an offense in Jesus' day as it was in ancient times and as it is today.

But listen as Jesus shifted the guilt of murder to the innermost realms of an angry heart: "But I say to you that everyone who is angry with his brother shall be guilty before the court" (v. 22). Most of us have not committed the legal act of murder; but lest any one of us thinks he's home free on the anger front, let's survey the range of words used in various translations of the Bible to describe "is angry."

+ *"harbor malice"*

    To harbor is to keep a thought or feeling, usually a negative one, secretly in one's mind, or to give a home or shelter to something. In our context, it is malice that we harbor.

+ *"become exasperated"*

    To become exasperated is to become intensely irritated or annoyed with someone or something, or to become infuriated.

+   *"enmity of heart"*

    Enmity is the state or feeling of being actively opposed or
    hostile to someone or something.

+   *"continues to be angry"*

    Continues to be angry implies anger that is firmly established
    at a deep or profound level; it's anger we're unwilling to lay
    aside. Deep-seated anger simmers like a cancer within us,
    and worse yet, we willfully feed that cancer.

Beginning to feel a little uncomfortable? Beloved, anger is a serious
deal! As harmless as we may have thought these types of anger to be, they
are, in fact, as serious in our hearts as actual murder. Jesus, who is the
fulfillment of God's law, zeroed in on the greater point: "I know what the
ancients said: if you commit a physical act of murder, you're responsible to
the court. But I say something much more difficult. The guilt of murder
begins long before the physical act. The guilt of murder begins in the
heart—with anger."

The playing field of sin is level. Sin is sin, whether it's murder or anger,
whether it's you or me. Angry people will stand in a heavenly courtroom
over which God presides as judge, and they will stand guilty before Him.
Do you wonder why Jesus judges the sin of anger so critically? There is
an answer, and it might not be what you think. Jesus takes anger seriously
because He knows its destructiveness—and He doesn't want anyone to
suffer the devastation of sin. Whether anger flashes within us or whether
it seethes, anger is a heart issue, one from which our all-wise heavenly
Father, in boundless compassion toward us, wants to set us free. Friend,
never despair. Jesus died for the sins of the world—for your sin and mine. In
Jesus, we find forgiveness and the strength to deal with anger.

There is another reason to seek and maintain freedom from anger.
Anger can destroy our Christian influence. If we're responsible to stop decay
in the world, and if we're responsible to lead people out of darkness to the
Light, then we must have good relationships with those around us. As a
pastor, I'm a student of people. In fact, the Bible teaches that I'm responsible
to know the condition of my church flock. Over the years, I've seen many
people ruin not only their personal and business relationships but also their
reputation. If we destroy our relationships and our reputation, we will never

be salt and light. Anger keeps us from influencing the world around us and from reflecting the character and light of Christ.

Do you remember Jesus' purpose for preaching the Sermon on the Mount? He was getting us ready for the blessed life, a life that is ready for any storm. It could be that the storm of anger has already invaded your life, or it may be that the storm of anger waits just on the horizon. Let's not fail to listen to and obey Jesus' teaching. For us to live as salt and light in this world, anger can have no place in our lives. Why should we look critically at the heart issue of anger? Just ask my friend Pete, serving a life sentence in the McAlester State Penitentiary, a place he never imagined anger would take him.

The Corruption of Anger

Have you ever declared (or mumbled) "you good-for-nothing"? Jesus continued His discourse on anger, this time examining our tongues as well as our hearts.

> And whoever says to his brother, "You good-for-nothing," shall
> be guilty before the supreme court; and whoever says, "You fool,"
> shall be guilty enough to go into the fiery hell. (Matthew 5:22)

The term *brother* in this verse is not a narrow term, restricted to a sibling, friend, or Christian brother or sister; instead, it is applied more broadly to include our brother the server at the local coffee shop, our sister the ticket agent at the airport, and our brother the annoyed driver honking impatiently behind us. Our brother is the person whose name we may never know but to whom we are ordained to be salt and light.

The phrase "good-for-nothing" is the Greek word *raca*. No English word translates exactly, but the idea is a brainless, worthless, empty-headed person. *The MacArthur New Testament Commentary* says *raca* can be translated "blockhead" (1985, 295). The "supreme court" refers to the Sanhedrin, the council of seventy learned men in Jesus' day who judged the most serious breaches of the Law, including handing down the death sentence. What was Jesus saying? "Good-for-nothing" (or the modern-day equivalent) is the verbal evidence of anger erupting from deep within our heart—and in the eyes of our Lord, it's as serious a sin as murder. Remember that the scribes and Pharisees strained to follow every iota of God's (and man's) law, and on the outside, they did a fine job. Yet, Jesus declared them "hypocrites." Why? Not their actions, but their hearts were corrupt to the core.

Now the lesson gets especially rough. "Whoever says, 'You fool,' shall be guilty enough to go into the fiery hell." Jesus was illustrating that no matter the display of anger—whether it's murder or calling someone "you blockhead"—the journey of anger is a trip the children of God should never take. Why? Because anger takes us where we never intended to go.

The Silence of Anger

As Jesus described salt-and-light living, He warned us again of the damaging effects of anger. Whether I'm angry with my brother, or the flipside—I'm not angry, but my brother has something against me—anger will not only negate our influence as salt and light to those around us but it will also silence our relationship with the Lord.

Now, please notice that I did not say anger *ends* our relationship with the Lord. It doesn't. Our salvation has never depended on our merit and it never will, for it is "by grace [we] have been saved through faith; and that not of [ourselves], *it is* the gift of God; not as a result of works, so that no one may boast" (Ephesians 2:8-9). Our salvation is perfect and complete in Christ's one-time sacrifice. No, anger does not end our relationship with God, but it does silence it. Let me explain as we look at Matthew 5:23-24.

> Therefore if you are presenting your offering at the altar, and there remember that your brother has something against you, leave your offering there before the altar and go; first be reconciled to your brother, and then come and present your offering.

Some years ago, I had been angry for weeks on end following a very difficult situation. During that time, a respected deacon came to my office and asked if he could share something important with me. As his pastor, I assured him that he could, because I wanted to minister to him and encourage him in any way possible. After his first few sentences, it became apparent that he hadn't come to talk with me about himself—he had come to talk with me about me. Here are the words he shared.

> I know you've walked through some very difficult days, and from a human standpoint, you may have the right to be angry. But, Pastor, if you're angry, then you cannot communicate with God; and if you cannot communicate with God, you will not be able to hear from Him. And if you cannot hear from God, then you cannot tell me what God wants to say to me when you preach on Sunday. Pastor, your ministry is too important for you to be angry. Will you please forgive? My spiritual life may be depending on it.

Have you ever been hit with a spiritual brick? May God bless those who love us enough to throw one our way. To that dear deacon (and you know who you are), thank you, my faithful brother.

"Therefore if you are presenting your offering at the altar." As modern-day Christians, we tend to think that "offering" refers to the money we give to the church. As a boy, I remember my parents asking me every Sunday before we left for church if I had remembered to bring "my offering." That meant, did I have with me the envelope the church had given me, and had I placed my money inside the envelope to "give my offering" that day at church? Now, as a pastor, it bothers me a little when we "take" the offering at church. Tell me, is it really an offering if we have to take it? Isn't an offering something we give willingly? After all, Jesus "offered" His life for us. He said that no one would "take" His life from Him because He would willingly lay it down. Friends, I hope the money we give to a church is not something someone "takes" from us; I pray that we give our offering willingly.

When Jesus said, "If you are presenting your offering at the altar," His point was not money. The subject of His sentence was "you." Some commentators suggest that Jesus was referring to the sacrifice offered on the Day of Atonement. On that day, a worshiper would give an animal to the temple priest, who then communicated with God on that person's behalf, asking God to forgive the sins of the worshiper. The priest would then lay his hand on the animal to indicate that the sins had been confessed and symbolically laid on the animal of sacrifice. Finally, the blood of the animal was spilled to cover the sins of that person. Because Jesus gave His life to atone for the sins of the world, there is no longer a need to offer imperfect sacrifices through a priest (see Galatians 1:3-5). If you will, the temple sacrifice was the coloring book outline; Jesus was the living-color completion of the atonement picture. Christ's sacrifice was perfect and final, and it opened the way for us to approach the altar of God ourselves.

So, when we go to worship before the Father, to seek God's blessing or direction, to confess sin, or to offer praise, we must make sure that we harbor no anger. Again, understanding the destructiveness of anger, Jesus said, "Leave your offering there before the altar and go; first be reconciled to your brother, and then come and present your offering." We read in Psalm 66:18, "If I regard wickedness in my heart, the Lord will not hear." The truth is, we cannot do business with God if we cling to anger.

My friend, *you* are too important to the work of God to harbor anger, and your communication with the Father is too important to be silenced. Jesus clearly communicated the seriousness and the consequences of anger, and we get it, don't we? Here's the good news. With us in mind, Jesus also graciously illustrated the path that leads out of destructive anger and into personal, spiritual, and relational peace, forgiveness, and reconciliation.

The Joy of a Reconciled Heart

For me, the fact that anger keeps us from communicating with the Lord is a dismal prospect, because in stormy situations, I need to be at His feet seeking wisdom, guidance, and who knows what else. So let's not get bogged down here. Instead, let's look carefully at the end of verse 24: "First be reconciled to your brother, and then come and present your offering."

To us, even the thought of trying to reconcile with an angry or wounded brother or sister makes us squirm. Not Jesus. He simply affirmed reconciling as a matter of practice and then continued on to the "come before Me" part. There must be something positive and good about being right (and attempting to be right) with our brother; so, when we need to deal with anger, let's not look at it as a dreadful thing that's certain to cause heartache. Just the opposite is true. Doing our part to reconcile a relationship simply makes us ready to do business with God, and that's a very good position in which to be. God willing, we will have a positive influence on our brother, sister, or even our enemy—and that would mean we are becoming salt and light. As with all things, we do our part under the guidance of the Holy Spirit, and then we leave the results to God.

The Joy of Freedom

There is one more reason Jesus gave for His children to stay free from anger. As I investigate these verses, it seems to me that anger keeps us from living free. Jesus' words in Matthew 5:25-26 are amazing. (My wife says I use the word *amazing* a lot, and that may be true; but I'm telling you, these words really are amazing!)

> Make friends quickly with your opponent at law while you are with him on the way, so that your opponent may not hand you over to the judge, and the judge to the officer and you be thrown into prison. Truly I say to you, you will not come out of there until you have paid up the last cent.

Jesus was referencing a common situation in His day. When two people were on their way to court to settle a difference, say, a financial dispute, it was important for them to settle the issue *before* they stood before the judge. Why? Because once the court was involved, the court, not the parties in dispute, would settle the problem. If a situation remained unresolved and was thus taken to court, the judge might just find both parties guilty, and the whole lot of them would soon find themselves to be prison cellmates. *They would lose their freedom*, and they would remain imprisoned until every cent was paid! The problem is that when you're in prison, you cannot pay even a cent on a debt.

Like prisoners in a jail, bound people are not free to move forward with their lives. They're stuck. The prison cells of anger are self-limiting; they offer little room to move around. Is there unsettled anger from your childhood that you'd like to be free of? Are you and your spouse bound by anger, unable to make progress in your relationship? Christ-followers have little freedom to walk with God when we harbor unsettled issues.

So, if God wants us to live free, for our own good and for the good of others, how will we be freed? The apostle Paul asked a similar question in Romans 7: "Who will release and deliver me from the shackles of this body of death?" (v. 24 AMP). With great relief, he also gave the answer: "O thank God! He will! through Jesus Christ our Lord!" (v. 25). Paul later gave practical instructions to the Christians in Colossae regarding the things that bind Christ's followers—put those things aside!

> And in them you also once walked, when you were living in them. But now you also, put them all aside: anger, wrath, malice, slander, and abusive speech from your mouth. Do not lie to one another, since you laid aside the old self with its evil practices, and have put on the new self who is being renewed to a true knowledge according to the image of the One who created him.
>
> So, as those who have been chosen of God, holy and beloved, put on a heart of compassion, kindness, humility, gentleness and patience; bearing with one another, and forgiving each other, whoever has a complaint against anyone; just as the Lord forgave you, so also should you. Beyond all these things put on love, which is the perfect bond of unity. Let the peace of Christ rule in your hearts, to which indeed you were called in one body; and be thankful. (Colossians 3:7-10, 12-15)

Put it aside, Paul said—even as a dirty garment—and keep putting it aside. Every time the dirty garment surfaces, say, "I can't wear that. It's not who I am." And that's true. As the apostle Paul said, we are "chosen of God, holy and beloved." So, beloved children of God, choose not to wear the dirty thing. Make putting it aside a habit. Then, "put on a heart of compassion, kindness, humility, gentleness and patience." Forgive, just as we've been forgiven. Let Christ rule in our hearts with peace, and be thankful.

Is this hard work? You bet it is. Is it a one-time event? Well, probably not. But the Spirit of the Living God, the Creator of all that's good, lives within us. Each time we "put aside" that harmful garment, its grip on us loosens. This difficult act requires the discipline of "taking every thought captive to the obedience of Christ" (2 Corinthians 10:5).

Storms of life do come, but we can stand firm in them. The blessed life is possible, but we must hear and obey. Influencing others for Christ is eternally important, so we must retain our saltiness. Light leads the lost and the blind out of darkness, and only we can reflect the Light of the world. "Putting aside" is difficult and perhaps a repetitive action, but freedom is worth it. You're worth it. Jesus knew so.

In teaching us to be salt and light in our relationships, Jesus turned His attention to the relationship of marriage. Whether you're married now, you used to be married, you want to be married, you know someone who is married, or you just have a relationship that's important to you, the Lord taught us about protecting our most prized relationships. It may well be one of the keys to living the blessed life.

Living It Out

1. According to chapter 5, dealing with anger allows us to have the _____ of a reconciled heart and the _____ of freedom.

2. Are you living in a prison cell of anger, bound by unforgiveness and hurt?

   Remember, you are too important to God and to others to silence His communication with you! If you're willing, ask God to help you forgive and even to reconcile with your brother or sister.

3. Are you ready to lay aside, once and for all, any sin (dirty garment) that threatens to destroy your witness for Christ?

   Make it your habit to put those old clothes aside, and clothe yourself instead with garments that identify you for who you really are—a child of the King, "chosen of God, holy and beloved" (Colossians 3:12).

Let's Pray

Father, thank You for showing me the freedom and joy that can be mine when I deal with sin in my life. Please give me the courage and the desire to lay aside, and keep laying aside, anger. I ask these things in the name of Jesus Christ. Amen.

6

Salt and Light in Marriage

Matthew 5:27-32

But I say to you that everyone who looks at a woman with lust for her
has already committed adultery with her in his heart.
—Matthew 5:28

I recently read a sign about marriage that is simply *not* true. It was the day I performed the marriage ceremony for a young couple from our church. The wedding took place in a beautiful setting about twenty-five miles from our home, a gorgeous wedding chapel in the wooded hills of northeastern Oklahoma. When my wife and I arrived at the chapel, I first walked into the area where the wedding would take place; then having a little time on our hands, Jerri and I walked to the room where the reception would be held. That's where I saw the offending sign. It hung above the archway through which couples walk as they're introduced as "Mr. and Mrs. So-and-So." The sign read, "And They Lived Happily Ever After." Happily ever after may work in fairy tales, but that notion is simply inaccurate concerning marriage. Don't get me wrong. I'm not saying marriage is unhappy, because marriage can be wonderful. But it is not, as if by some magic *pwang!* of a wand, "happily ever after." The truth is that marriage is work.

Over our forty-plus years together, Jerri and I have worked at our marriage, though "work" doesn't mean our marriage has been difficult.

It means that we have actively and purposefully *worked at* our marriage. At times, we've had to apologize to one other, and on occasion, we've needed to adjust our priorities or change our plans to accommodate the other. Nevertheless, every conscious effort to protect this most important of relationships has been well worth the work, and for many reasons, but especially as we've sought to influence those around us through our marriage, as salt and light.

As we continue to build our life and witness on a firm foundation, and as we seek to live the blessed life, let's draw from the Sermon on the Mount three habits that will protect our most valued relationships. Each habit is given in the form of a commitment. Sound like work? Just hang in there with me. Before you throw a hymnbook my way, hear me out to the end, because when you finish the last word of this chapter, you will be able to respond wholeheartedly to all three commitments by saying, "I can do that!" And as you read this chapter, don't let the devil discourage or condemn you. No matter who you are—a spouse, a parent, a single person, a friend, a Christ-follower, an employee—you will eagerly say, "With God's help, I can make those commitments."

Ready? Let's get to work!

Commitments that Protect

Christ-followers, living as salt and light in this world, must protect their marriages and relationships. Here is the first commitment.

COMMITMENT ONE

I commit to let Jesus' truths trump the lies of the world

Jesus reminded His disciples, and thereby reminds us, of what "was said" concerning adultery.

> You have heard that it was said, "You shall not commit adultery."
> (Matthew 5:27)

Obviously, Jesus was quoting from the Ten Commandments, which were given by God sometime around 1447 B.C. and are recorded in Exodus 20. "You shall not commit adultery," reads the seventh commandment. No doubt the disciples knew this commandment, and many today know it too. But allow me the interpretive license to apply what "was said" to contemporary society: "You have heard that it was said at one time in America, 'You shall not commit adultery.'"

Do we still hear that command? The entertainment media doesn't say, "You shall not." No, it encourages immorality and glorifies adultery. What do we see or hear from our sports "heroes"? From the news media? The education world? Do we regularly hear biblical truth, or do we hear lies? Young people used to be taught, "Hands off!" Today's youth, to the contrary, are bombarded with images and information that not only encourage sexual activity before marriage but also portray sex as merely a normal part of dating life. In our upside-down world, anyone who is faithful in marriage or pure before marriage is considered strange. Clearly, our world tends to disregard this vital, protective truth against adultery; after all, sex sells. The destructive lies of the world—the storm of sexual sin—rages against the family.

Once Jesus reminded His disciples of the divine truth that commanded us not to commit adultery, He actually moved that truth to its highest level. He raised the bar. He spoke beyond our actions to address our most private thoughts, and here's where the work of protecting comes in.

> You have heard that it was said, "You shall not commit adultery";
> but I say to you that everyone who looks at a woman with lust
> for her has already committed adultery with her in his heart.
> (Matthew 5:27-28)

The word "I" in verse 28 is emphatic. Jesus was saying, "You have heard what the law commands; now *I* make that law complete by saying that to even *look* at a woman (or man) with lust is to commit adultery in your heart."

If you come into my office and I show you a photograph of my daughter's wedding, I might say to you, "Just *look* at that cute couple!" That usage is not the "look" used in verse 28. Jesus was referring to a long, contemplative look. A mental vision type of look, one that moves into impurity. This look might be toward the cover of a magazine, an Internet page, an adult television channel, the big screen of a movie theater, and certainly a lingering look toward someone other than your spouse.

Remember the tragic story of King David and Bathsheba (2 Samuel 11)? Their adulterous involvement began with a lingering look. One evening, while viewing the city from his palace rooftop, David noticed a woman bathing. Had he immediately turned away, the story could have been different, but the Bible tells us that he saw her, and he lingered at what he saw. *Saw* in Hebrew actually means "to look closely" or "to examine." David examined this woman, and his long, lingering look urged him toward immorality. The storm erupted because David did not protect his marriage, and the consequences were great.

Today's world says go ahead, commit adultery. Jesus said, "Do not." The world says sex outside of marriage is harmless; after all, it's just a natural part of life. Jesus said, "Do not." The world tells women and girls to dress however they choose. Jesus said we're all responsible to consider whether our clothing could tempt someone to take a long, contemplative look.

My friend, you and I have a commitment to make. If we're going to protect our most important relationships, then we must commit *to let Jesus' truths trump the lies of the world*. Depending every moment on God for strength, let's respond right now with an eager, "I can do that!"

COMMITMENT TWO

I commit to make my marriage my most prized possession

After Jesus equated "looks at a woman with lust" with actual adultery (5:27-28), He then gave two shocking, nearly unfathomable statements:

> If your right eye makes you stumble, tear it out and throw it from you; for it is better for you to lose one of the parts of your body, than for your whole body to be thrown into hell. (Matthew 5:29)

> If your right hand makes you stumble, cut it off and throw it from you; for it is better for you to lose one of the parts of

your body, than for your whole body to go into hell.
(Matthew 5:30)

What in the world could Jesus have meant? Are we to take these statements literally? Do we ignore them as ridiculous? Perhaps this information will clear the picture. When interpreting biblical texts, we can take a text literally *unless* taking it literally would be absurd or would disregard the rest of the Bible. For example, Jesus publicly proclaimed, "I am the door" (John 10:9). Was Jesus really a chunk of wood? Of course not. That would be an absurd interpretation. By using this figure of speech, Jesus was simply saying, "I am the way, the path, the only access to salvation."

Good news. In the same way, Jesus was not instructing us to carry out a violent, external act of self-harm (as if that would solve an issue of the heart). Remember, He spoke beyond our actions to address our most private thoughts. To paraphrase, Jesus was instead saying, "Your hand and eye are vitally important to your health and well-being. So if anything tempts you to violate the sanctity of your eye or hand, stop! Stop immediately, and drastically cut out that thing that could cause you harm. Hurl it from you now!"

A contemporary application of this truth? Jesus might say to us today, "Immoral thoughts and behavior, sex outside of marriage, pornography, [fill in the blank with any impurity]—these things have no place in your life. They are *not* more important than a pure life and a pure marriage. They are *not* more important than an unbroken relationship with Me. Stop these things immediately! *Your marriage, like your right eye or hand, is your most prized possession.* Protect it. Drastically cut out that thing that is causing or could cause you harm. Cut it away from you immediately!"

The word *stumble* is vital to the wisdom of Jesus' narrative. "If your right eye makes you stumble, tear it out and throw it from you," and, "If your right hand makes you stumble, cut it off and throw it far from you." Stumble actually refers to a "bait-stick." Remember Elmer Fudd holding a string attached to a stick that held up the ACME box, staging a trap for Bugs Bunny? Lured by the carrot under the box, Bugs predictably ventured into the trap. Elmer would then pull the bait-stick, attempting to capture Bugs in the ACME box. In life, the allure of carrots is inescapable. Many opportunities to see or to do are in reality traps. Again, Jesus said watch out for the bait-stick! Whatever causes you to stumble, violently cast it from you—no matter the loss or pain involved in the casting.

So, how do we make marriage our most prized possession? Several years ago, I dropped by the home of Steve and Lisa, a young couple who had visited our church. I noticed on the mantel of their fireplace a small, clear case that held several championship rings. Being an admirer of athletes, I asked Steve about the rings. He explained that he had won the first ring as an all-state player in high school, and he won the second ring playing for the University of Tulsa when they won a conference championship. As I was admiring the rings, Lisa asked if I would like to see his Super Bowl ring! "What? Absolutely yes!" She walked to another room and soon returned holding securely in her grip a metal lockbox. With great care, this adoring wife unlocked the box and took out a velvet ring box. As she opened the velvet box, I saw the most majestic ring I have ever seen. This symbol of excellence flashed with gold and brilliant diamonds. Steve had played one particular year in the NFL—and that year the team won the Super Bowl.

Now here's the point. This young couple prized that magnificent, hard-won ring, and they were delighted to show it off. They were vigilant to protect the ring from theft and harm by keeping it securely locked and in a safe place. With great care, Lisa had carried the Super Bowl ring tightly in her grip. Just as this couple painstakingly protected this prized possession, so we must also give our marriage the protection it deserves as a valuable, God-given treasure.

There's a wonderful postscript to this story. Jerri and I were recently at a Christmas gathering for pastors and their wives when, to our surprise, a couple greeted us and introduced themselves. It was Lisa and Steve. We hadn't seen them in many years, and our reunion was delightful. As we caught up with their lives, they told us that Steve is now a bi-vocational pastor! Not only have Steve and Lisa protected the memories of his glowing football career but they have also continued to protect their marriage. Championship rings are amazing, but the greatest championship win for Steve and Lisa is a protected marriage, a prized possession symbolized by the rings they wear on their left hands.

Are you ready to say "Yes!" to Jesus' admonition to make your marriage your most prized possession? Lest the commitment seem overwhelming, listen carefully to Matthew 19:26: "And looking at them Jesus said to them, 'With men this is impossible, but with God all things are possible.'" Jesus is looking at you and me, saying to us as well, "With God, all things are possible." We simply respond, "Lord, with Your great help, we commit to treasure our spouse and make marriage our most prized possession, beginning today."

COMMITMENT THREE

I will refuse to take something God made beautiful and make it hellish

We have one final discipline to explore as we learn to protect our most prized relationship. Hang with me. It will be worth it!

Thus far, Jesus' truths regarding impurity have been sobering enough. Still, He gave not once, but twice, a stern warning that makes the hair on your neck stand up. See what you think.

> For it is better for you to lose one of the parts of your body, than for your whole body to be thrown into hell. If your right hand makes you stumble, cut it off and throw it from you; for it is better for you to lose one of the parts of your body, than for your whole body to go into hell. (Matthew 5:29-30)

Did you catch those statements about hell? Many of us have been Christians for so long, we may have forgotten that we are saved *from hell*. We are saved from eternal torment, from pain and fire. We are saved from the eternal memory of knowing we rejected Jesus. Eternity with God "in heaven" is our certain future. But my Christian friend, we can create our own hell on earth. Adultery—and the consequences of adultery—is hellish! No-nonsense Jesus unmasked the world's lie by saying adultery is like going to hell. It is neither blissful nor better, as the world makes it appear. It is hellish. And, sex outside of marriage is not beautiful, or pure, or heavenly. The apostle Paul put it all into perspective.

> Do you not know that your bodies are members of Christ? Shall I then take away the members of Christ and make them members of a prostitute? May it never be! Or do you not know that the one who joins himself to a prostitute is one body with her? For He says, "The two shall become one flesh."

> But the one who joins himself to the Lord is one spirit with
> Him. Flee immorality. Every other sin that a man commits is
> outside the body, but the immoral man sins against his own body.
> Or do you not know that your body is a temple of the Holy
> Spirit who is in you, whom you have from God, and that you are
> not your own? For you have been bought with a price: therefore
> glorify God in your body. (1 Corinthians 6:15-20)

Notice Paul's clear directive: "Flee immorality." If doing or seeing
something could cause us to take something God made beautiful and make
it hellish, we must stop seeing that thing, we must stop doing that thing.
Remove it from us. Remove us from it, immediately and abruptly. Don't
ease out of it—stop now!

In stark contrast to the self-induced hell of immorality, marriage is a
beautiful concept rooted in God's heart.

+ John the Baptist spoke of Jesus Christ as "the bridegroom"
  (John 3:29).

+ The apostle Paul told the church in Corinth, "I betrothed
  you to one husband, that to Christ I might present you" (2
  Corinthians 11:2).

+ John, the beloved apostle of Jesus, described the future
  heavenly marriage of the Bridegroom to His bride, the
  church: "Let us rejoice and be glad and give the glory to
  Him, for the marriage of the Lamb has come and His bride
  has made herself ready" (Revelation 19:7-10).

From the hell of immorality to the blessing of a life purely lived, the
message is clear. Yes, we can choose to ignore Jesus' commands 1) to protect
the sanctity, health, and well-being of our most valued relationship, 2) to
drastically cut out that thing that causes us to stumble, and 3) to cut it
away immediately—but we ignore them to our own peril. Rather than
paying the terrible price of disregarding these truths, we must refuse to take
something God made beautiful and make it hellish.

As we live as Christ's salt and light on earth, protecting our most valued
relationship requires that we actively and purposefully *work at* our marriage.

But it is worth it, both now and for eternity. Depending every moment on God's strength, it is more than doable. Ready? Let's get to work!

An Interlude of Grace: God Forgives

Right about now, we may need to take a break. Have you made some mistakes concerning marriage, perhaps involving sin? The eternal truth is that God is a God of grace and forgiveness. Whether you've gone through marriage difficulties or even a divorce, please read the next few paragraphs carefully. There is good news for you.

Although labels are most generally negative and unhelpful, like it or not, we all carry at least one of the following "marital status" labels:

+ married
+ getting married
+ remarried
+ divorced
+ getting divorced
+ contemplating divorce

+ never married
+ contemplating marriage
+ married to a previously divorced person
+ adulterous (not a term used on a form with a checkbox beside it)

Once again, let me say to all that no matter your current "label," I, Ted Kersh, choose to be a person of grace, so I want you to relax. My Christian brothers and sisters, Jesus is not interested in beating you up. Quite the opposite is true. He cares for us, and He is ever full of grace, ready to forgive.

Years ago, following a grace-leaning sermon I preached on divorce and immorality, a man came to me and said, "Well, Preacher, you really missed that deal!" Before I could open my mouth to respond, he continued with a seething, Pharisaical rant: "Yep. *You, a preacher, should know* that God hates divorce. Somebody needs to tell those folks that *God hates divorce!*" With a good measure of self-restraint (I tried anyway), I spoke the following truth: "Yes sir, I know God hates divorce. We all hate the devastation of divorce. But I also know that Proverbs 6:19 says, God hates the 'one who spreads strife among brothers!'" Kind of a writing-in-the-dirt moment, don't you think (see John 8:4-7)?

To those who tend toward legalism rather than grace, I want you to know that I am fully aware that God said in Malachi 2:16, "I hate divorce." The truth is that God hates *all* sin. Why, because He's an angry God who hates sinners? Absolutely not! Conversely, because God's love toward us is limitless and pure, He hates the sin that devastates our lives.

I'm amazed that we in the church will forgive the sin of murder before we will forgive the sin of divorce. Far too often, we take the position of un-grace toward certain sins we deem to be the bad ones. Shame on us. Whether the sin is murder, or divorce, or strife, God forgives repentant sinners! All sin can be forgiven. According to 1 John 1:9, "If we confess our sins, He is faithful and righteous to forgive us our sins and to cleanse us from all unrighteousness." My fellow sinner, we run to the cross where the blood of Jesus was shed for all sin. The cross is a place of grace and safety, not of legalism. Divorce and every other sin can be confessed and cleansed.

On the other hand, do we presume upon God's grace and forgiveness by continuing in sin? Of course not! Or, as the apostle Paul put it, "Are we to continue in sin that grace might increase? May it never be!" (Romans 6:1-2). But we as sinners have the comfort of knowing that when we do sin and repent of that sin, God's love, forgiveness, and grace abound (Romans 5:20).

Whatever label you wear, God is interested in the marriage you have today. He's more interested in where you're going with your marriage than in where you've been. Through the rest of this chapter, please do not let the Evil One bring condemnation your way. Instead, allow God to love on you. Allow His blessed truth to instruct you for today and for the future—to make certain the marriage you're in today is all God intends it to be. I pray you read the final word of this chapter and say, "I'm so glad God is a God of grace!"

The High Value of a Godly Marriage

At this point in our discussion on living in this world as salt and light, I pray for you the following:

+ That you see the benefits of "working at" your marriage.

+ That you're inspired to make those three marriage-protecting commitments.

+ That you've run to Christ's cross to receive His gracious offer of forgiveness.

+ That you now wear the label "Forgiven!"

Now, let's briefly explore and willingly embrace the deep and lasting values of a marriage built on the Rock. In Matthew 5:31, Jesus once again reminded His disciples of what "was said":

> It was said, "Whoever sends his wife away, let him give her a certificate of divorce"; but I say to you that everyone who divorces his wife, except for the reason of unchastity, makes her commit adultery; and whoever marries a divorced woman commits adultery. (Matthew 5:31-32)

Jesus was quoting from Deuteronomy 24:1-4, when Moses said that if a man married a woman and she found no favor in his eyes, he could not simply send her away. Instead, he had to first write for her a certificate of divorce, put it in her hand, and then he could send her away. Some Pharisees asked Jesus (see Matthew 19) why Moses allowed such a process. Jesus' answer? "Because of your hardness of heart" (19:8). The cultural view was that if a man sent a woman away without a certificate of divorce, it was assumed that she had committed adultery. At the most, she could face death; at the least, her reputation was ruined.

In Jesus' day, men sent their wives away for anything they thought was indecent, and there's evidence they even divorced for things such as burning the toast! They were divorcing for any reason at all. Sounds like our day, doesn't it? Marriage then and now is too often viewed as a mere legal arrangement that can be easily terminated. When one party no longer wants to maintain the contract, the spouse is divorced. The only problem is that in God's eyes, marriage is much more than a legal contract; it is a covenantal agreement. So, what makes marriage so valuable to God's plans and purposes?

Marriage Removes Our Aloneness

God, the blessed Creator of all things, including marriage, explained one purpose for marriage. "Then the LORD God said, 'It is not good for the man to be alone; I will make him a helper suitable for him'" (Genesis 2:18). When God created the universe, the world, and everything therein, He proclaimed that all He created was "good." He made a different pronouncement, however, concerning Adam: "It is not good for the man to be alone." Therefore, God created Eve. He created marriage, the joining of one man to one woman, to remove our aloneness. We marry to go through life together, not alone.

I mentioned previously that Jerri and I have been married for more than forty years. You cannot go through forty years of marriage without experiencing storms, and a strong marriage is necessary for navigating life's storms. I have been Jerri's rock, and she has been my soft place where I can run. There have been times when we had only each other. There have been days when no one would stand with me except Jerri. Many times only Jerri knew my heartache, because as a pastor, I often can turn only to my wife. Jerri and I know storms. But God gave us the blessing of marriage. We cleave to one other. We are one flesh. Jerri is my God-given helpmate. God fashioned her just for me. With Jerri, I'm never alone. What a "good" deal! God gave us marriage to remove our aloneness. I bless Him for that.

Marriage: A Path to Spiritual Growth

While we celebrate our anniversary with each passing year, Jerri and I never stop "reaching forward to what lies ahead" (Philippians 3:13-14). We resist the temptation to pat ourselves on the back and say, "Good going! With forty years under our belts, we've now arrived." No. God says, "Where are you going with your marriage? Where are you headed?"

So, here's another purpose for marriage: our marriages must be a path for spiritual growth. In Matthew 5:32, Jesus gave us one of the two reasons that divorce is acceptable—adultery: "But I say to you that everyone who divorces his wife, except for the reason of unchastity, makes her commit adultery; and whoever marries a divorced woman commits adultery." The apostle Paul gave the other reason in 1 Corinthian 7:15: "If the unbelieving one leaves, let him leave; the brother or the sister is not under bondage in such cases, but God has called us to peace." From these verses, we see that adultery is obviously a result of someone's spiritual decline. One thing Jesus was teaching in this passage is that, rather than marriage being a place of mere survival or even of spiritual decline, marriage can be a path for spiritual growth. The role of Christian husbands and Christian wives is to take their marriages down a path that produces spiritual growth within their family, their church, and their world.

Let me say it this way. Men, you are to be in such a place spiritually that you can help and encourage your wife toward spiritual progress. That should be your desire, your priority, and your habit. Your wife should know that you pray for her and will readily pray with her about any concern. Your wife should look more like Jesus *because she lives with you.* The apostle Paul said it beautifully.

> Husbands, love your wives, as Christ loved the church and gave Himself up for her. . . . Even so husbands should love their wives as [being in a sense] their own bodies. He who loves his own wife loves himself. For no man ever hated his own flesh, but nourishes and carefully protects and cherishes it, as Christ does the church. (Ephesians 5:25, 28-29 AMP)

Men, what wife could turn away from such love? If you will love your wife as Christ loved the church, and if you will give yourself for her, then there will be no problem with her responding to you as to the Lord. That type of marriage is far more than a legal contract; it is divorce proof.

Ladies, the apostle Paul also gave the following instructions:

> Wives, be subject (be submissive and adapt yourselves) to your own husbands, as a service to the Lord. . . . Let the wife see that she respects and reverences her husband [that she notices him, regards him, honors him, prefers him, venerates, and esteems him; and that she defers to him, praises him, and loves and admires him exceedingly]. (Ephesians 5:22, 33 AMP)

Wow! What husband could turn away from such love? Wives, your husband's spiritual growth will be enhanced as you love him, admire him, pray for him, and depend on him. Always expect spiritual growth, and he will be more likely to meet that expectation. This truth in itself will protect and even save many marriages.

✦ ✦ ✦

I'm glad you've stuck with me through this chapter. We've heard some difficult, yet loving truths, all spoken to encourage us to live as salt and light in our most valuable of relationships. Are we willing to take an honest look at our lives and ask, "Am I living as salt and light?" God's truths are alive and operative, and if we choose to follow them, they work. If we neglect them, then nothing works. With God's help, we can make these three commitments, now and every day hence. Are you ready? Let's get to work!

In the next chapter, we'll identify several practical, but not-so-easy habits that mark the life of a maturing Christian. By the way, are you a maturing believer?

Living It Out

1. From chapter 6, list the three commitments that will protect your marriage.

    1.

    2.

    3.

2. If you're willing, how can you implement each of the three commitments?

    Are you willing to work at them, even if your spouse doesn't?

    Will you trust God to help you?

3. By God's design, the love between a husband and wife is to reflect the love of Jesus (the Bridegroom) for His bride (the church). Knowing this, are you willing to "work at" building your marriage, with the goal of portraying to others Christ's love for the church?

Let's Pray

> *Father, today I make these three commitments to my spouse and to You. Please remind me every day of my responsibility to build and protect my marriage. I ask these things in the name of Jesus Christ. Amen.*

7

Salt and Light Habits of a Maturing Believer

Matthew 5:33-48

"Therefore you are to be perfect, as your heavenly Father is perfect."
—Matthew 5:48

S ometimes every word in a sentence is clear and understandable, but the concept formed by the combination of words isn't so clear. For example, consider this statement: "Christ-followers are to live every day as the salt of the earth and the light of the world." Each word is clear enough, right? It's certainly an easy statement to make, but perhaps the day-to-day, boots-on-the-ground reality is a bit more difficult to nail down. And to be honest, it sounds churchy and vague anyway. In this chapter, we try to firm up this jello-y idea. What exactly does living as salt and light look like practically, today, as you and I encounter colleagues, clients, and cashiers?

Let's start by remembering that salty people influence others for Christ; light-reflecting people draw others to Christ. Living as salt and light is simply *all about Christ* and His renown! As the prophet Isaiah said, "Our heartfelt desire is for Your name and for the remembrance of You" (Isaiah 26:8 AMP). Our greatest desire, as followers of Christ, is to make Him known, to shine the spotlight on the only Savior—so that the souls we encounter might come into a saving, personal relationship with the Light of the world. That's truth number one. Every day, you and I live as salt and light *in order to draw others to the living Christ.*

Truth two? For us to live as salt and light, we must be maturing believers in Christ. Notice that I said *maturing* believers, not *matured* believers. Truthfully, I've never met a matured believer. On this earth, no one has totally "arrived" in his or her Christian walk. (What a relief to know and a surprise to some!) No one has completed the process. As long as we live on this earth, we must be about the process of maturing—*so that* we can live as salt and light. Here is some good news. Wherever we are in our walk with the Lord—new followers of Christ, long-time followers, I'm-ready-to-get-serious followers—we can mature in Christ. That's what Jesus' Sermon on the Mount (and this book) is all about.

If "maturing," not perfection, is our goal, then why did Jesus give this staggering command: "Therefore you are to be perfect, as your heavenly Father is perfect" (Matthew 5:48). Be perfect? What can that mean? Well, as a pastor, I've spent my entire ministry telling people we are *not* perfect and never will be perfect! After all, that's why Jesus came to earth, to save us because we are imperfect; if we were perfect, then we would have no need for a Savior. But we're not. We are born with a sin nature, and we absolutely do need a Savior. That's why John the Baptist declared at the sight of Jesus, "Behold, the Lamb of God who takes away the sin of the world!" (John 1:29). What then is Jesus talking about when He says, "Be perfect"?

To be certain, turning from sin is our active posture, but the word *perfect* Jesus used has a much grander meaning. He was telling us "to be fulfilled," "to be complete," "to grow into fullness," and even "to grow into our identity." Some describe *perfect* in verse 48 as a circle, which is by definition a round-shaped figure that is complete, or perfect. Others say it describes a boy growing into manhood. I like that. Here's how *The Message* says it:

> In a word, what I'm saying is, Grow up. You're kingdom subjects. Now live like it. Live out your God-created identity. Live generously and graciously toward others, the way God lives toward you. (Matthew 5:48)

You and I can do that. We can, by the Holy Spirit, be always growing, always maturing, always "living generously and graciously toward others."

Every day, we can grow to look more like our Father, who is merciful, loving, forgiving, good, kind, just, wise, and faithful. We can make it our habit, day by day, to speak and act more like God. Why would we bother? Because others deserve it? No, they often don't—but neither do we. Nevertheless, even when we don't deserve it, *that's how God lives toward us!*

So let's return to our original question. What does living as salt and light actually look like? What qualities, habits, and attitudes in us will turn the spotlight on Jesus Christ? Beginning in Matthew 5:33, Jesus identified some practical habits of maturing believers, all of which display to others the character and ways of Christ.

Maturing Believers Develop Consistency of Character

One of the great challenges of living the Christian life is living it consistently. I wish it were so, but receiving the salvation Jesus offers does not instantly make us the picture of stellar, unwavering saints. No, it's not easy to always walk in the Spirit (see Galatians 5:16). There are times when my Christian character soars; other times, I regretfully act or speak something other than Christ-like. Nevertheless, my great desire as a maturing believer is to *develop* a consistent Christian character.

Consistency of character develops over time, step by step, day by day, as we surrender more of ourselves to the control of the Holy Spirit. If you and I live a "consistent" Christian life, then our thoughts, words, and actions will increasingly be described in the following ways:

+ steady
+ stable
+ dependable
+ reliable

+ unchanging
+ constant
+ free of contradictions
+ undeviating

In many areas of life, success depends on consistency. A winning football team, for instance, runs a play over and again in practice to develop the ability to make the play work in a game. Saving money requires consistency.

The amount put aside each week or month may not be as important; the idea is to keep saving, and one day, the savings account will have grown or "matured" to the point that it's useful. The same is true in the Christian life. We must develop consistency of character.

In Matthew 5:33, Jesus reminded His listeners of a law found in the Old Testament books of Leviticus, Numbers, and Deuteronomy.

> Again, you have heard that the ancients were told, "You shall not make false vows, but shall fulfill your vows to the lord."

Apparently, the religious leaders of Jesus' day had distorted this law (surprise, surprise). Here's how their version went: "If we use the name of God in an oath, then we're obligated to fulfill the terms of that oath; but, if we don't use God's name in the vow, then it's not *really* a vow; therefore, we don't have to keep our word." In other words, they were making excuses for their inconsistency. Their word lacked the character quality of integrity. But Jesus called His disciples to a higher standard of living. In verses 34-37, He set forth specific habits by which maturing believers can demonstrate consistency of character.

> But I say to you, make no oath at all, either by heaven, for it is the throne of God, or by earth, for it is the footstool of His feet, or by Jerusalem for it is the city of the great king. Nor shall you make an oath by your head, for you cannot make one hair white or black. But let your statement be, "Yes, yes" or "No, no"; anything beyond these is of evil. (Matthew 5:34-37)

Jesus' teaching on integrity can be summed up this way: the words and actions of Christ-followers are to be consistent. Special words are never required for us to keep our word or to make our words true. We strive to tell the truth the first time and to keep our word every time. With a simple "yes" or "no," everyone knows our words are true and reliable. We seek to neither speak rashly nor to take our words lightly in order to avoid any doubt as to the integrity of our character. What's more, our words are heard by our all-knowing God who (by the way) doesn't need to hear the sworn "by God" to know the truth. Above any other, He is our audience. In fact, adding God's name to what should be spoken truly in the first place misuses God's name.

Jesus' teaching is as clear as a bell, and it's a great challenge indeed. You may be thinking, "I can never be consistent. I'm always falling in my Christian walk. I guess I'll never be a maturing believer." Remember, you and I are *maturing* believers. Here's something I don't have trouble with: I am determined to *consistently strive to be consistent* in my walk with the Lord. The Lord knows our hearts. He watches not for perfection, but for growth in our character and integrity. My friends, with the help of God's indwelling Holy Spirit, we can *develop* a consistent Christian character, step by step, day by day.

Maturing Believers Meet Evil with God-Like Grace

Maturing believers view others' deeds—whether intentionally evil or merely inconvenient—as opportunities to demonstrate grace.

> You have heard that it was said, "An eye for an eye, and a tooth for a tooth." But I say to you, do not resist an evil person; but whoever slaps you on your right cheek, turn the other to him also. If anyone wants to sue you and take your shirt, let him have your coat also. (Matthew 5:38-42)

Jesus was quoting the civil law of retribution from Exodus 21: "An eye for an eye, and a tooth for a tooth." The law went on to say a burn for a burn and a fracture for a fracture, specifying that the punishment was to be equal to the crime, even to the point of a death for a death. (The law of retribution is alive and well today, isn't it? The world would undoubtedly say, "Go ahead, meet evil with evil, insult for insult. Get in their face, and make sure you get in the last word!") But Jesus interrupted this thought with His own standard: "Do not resist an evil person." In other words, "Do not set yourself against an evil person; instead, demonstrate the same grace that God extends. Meet every evil deed with grace!"

Responding in grace means not giving people who offend us what they deserve. We want God to deal justly with others, don't we? "Get 'um God!" That works fine until we want God to grant us mercy, not justice, for our evil deeds. The truth is that no one deserves God's grace; grace by definition is the undeserved favor of God. And yet, in spite of our sin, He gives grace freely. Jesus was saying, "To those by whose hand you suffer harm, respond not with retaliation, but with God's grace."

Then Jesus gave some specific examples of demonstrated grace. "But whoever slaps you on your right cheek, turn the other to him also" (v. 39). To slap someone on the cheek, especially on the right cheek, was to take away his or her dignity. This was a real "slap at one's dignity." Our natural reaction to such an act would be, "Dude, you just slapped the wrong guy!" Now, please hear me when I say that it is healthy and sometimes necessary to set and protect physical, spiritual, emotional, and mental boundaries. At the same time, maturing believers see conflict and offense through kingdom eyes—as opportunities to respond as salt and light. The apostle Paul explained it this way:

> If possible, so far as it depends on you, be at peace with all men. Never take your own revenge, beloved, but leave room for the wrath of God, for it is written, "Vengeance is mine, I will repay," says the Lord. "But if your enemy is hungry, feed him, and if he is thirsty, give him a drink; for in so doing you will heap burning coals on his head." (Romans 12:18-20)

Rather than retaliate, grace responds to offense humbly, *as if* turning the other cheek.

In another illustration of applied grace, Jesus said, "And if anyone wants to sue you and take your shirt, let him have your coat also" (v. 40). In Jesus' day, garments functioned as more than just clothing. For many people, garments were literally all they had for covering, so to lose their garments could mean they were exposed to the elements. For others, garments revealed their position in life: priestly garments identified a priest, and a judge's robe identified a judge. For these, the loss of garments symbolized the loss of their position in society, the loss of their security. "Let him have your coat also" was Jesus' way of saying, "I'm the Provider of your needs. So even in the midst of losing your security, respond with grace. You can trust Me to care for you."

Next, we read in verses 41 and 42 that maturing believers respond with grace in the face of inconvenience.

> Whoever forces you to go one mile, go with him two. Give to
> him who asks of you, and do not turn away from him who wants
> to borrow from you.

Now Jesus spoke to where we really live. You and I may never lose our dignity or even our security, but every one of us has been inconvenienced. How many times have we turned the car around because one child or another left a needed schoolbook at home? Or, have you noticed a cashier at the grocery store who is as slow as a slug, especially when you're in a rush? And of course, there's always a knucklehead with twenty-one items in the twenty-item checkout lane! Or, when on our way to work, driving the same road we always take, our way is blocked by a detour sign? This might be my response: "No one told *me* they were closing this road! Don't they know that I drive it every day? The highway department should have informed the tax-paying public of this disruption!"

One of the most inconvenient places on earth is the church, don't you agree? The *right* doors are never open (*right* being a respective term, referring to the door closest to your car and mine). The temperature inside the sanctuary is too cold—unless it's winter, and then it's too hot. Those seminary graduates, can they not work a thermostat? How much education does it take to keep a room the *correct* temperature? (Of course, *correct* is a differential term, relative to the number of people present.) And can't those sound booth "experts" hear that the music is too loud? That preacher, he keeps us here past noon—which is why I put my coat on during the invitation, I'll have you know. People should *not* make decisions for Christ after 11:45 AM.

How do you and I handle inconvenience? Jesus told His disciples, "Whoever forces you to go one mile, go with him two." He was referencing a serious situation faced by the Jews of His day. A Roman soldier had the legal right to force a Jew to carry equipment for one mile. This was more than just a little inconvenience in the mind of a Jew, who considered the Romans to be pagan invaders. It was downright demeaning. Yet, Jesus called

His disciples to demonstrate decisive grace when faced with the opportunity to serve as salt and light. Might such a situation be inconvenient? Yes. Uncomfortable? Probably. For an eternal purpose? You bet.

Many years ago, I went on an evangelistic visit one evening with a man from a church I served. We knocked on the door of a house, and when the homeowner opened the door, I noticed his sudden look of astonishment. We talked for a few minutes, but it was obvious we were not going to be invited inside. As we stepped off the porch, my friend confessed, "That was my fault, Preacher." When I questioned his remark, he explained that the man we just visited had been in my friend's retail business that very day. They had disagreed about the price of an item, and my church friend was rude to the man and had actually escorted him out of his store. My friend's demonstration of un-grace closed the door on that opportunity.

You and I have done the same thing, haven't we? When faced with the opportunity to influence someone toward Christ, we sometimes fail to handle the situation with grace. Friends, I understand that withholding retaliation runs counter to every fiber of our being, and even more so responding with grace to offense, conflict, loss, or inconvenience. Nevertheless, ours is to simply obey, leaving the rest in God's capable hands. What God does with the situation is frankly not our concern; it's His business. Our part is to live as salt and light and to respond with grace.

Remember, we grow into our identity as children of God, displaying His character for His glory. *O God, give us kingdom eyes to recognize evil and inconvenience as opportunities to display Your grace.*

Maturing Believers See Enemies as Opportunities

This habit is a tough one, but when practiced, it displays the type of courage and love that only God can give.

> You have heard that it was said, "YOU SHALL LOVE YOUR NEIGHBOR and hate your enemy." But I say to you, love your enemies and pray for those who persecute you. (Matthew 5:43-44)

Did you notice that "YOU SHALL LOVE YOUR NEIGHBOR" is set in uppercase letters, while the rest of the verse is lowercase? As you know, uppercase words are a quote from the Old Testament, in this case Leviticus 19:18, where God commanded that we reflect His own attribute of love to others. Conversely, the lowercase phrase "hate your enemy" was probably added by the fraudulent religious leaders of Jesus' day, giving themselves a convenient clause to opt-out of God's divine law. But Jesus once again turned wrong thinking right-side up when He stamped the "hate-your-enemy" pass INVALID and reaffirmed God's "love-your-neighbor" law.

With that, Jesus asked of His followers something most of us find difficult, if not nearly impossible: "Love your enemies and pray for those who persecute you." Really, Jesus? Love our neighbor *and* our enemy? Pray for the souls of those who ridicule Christians? Plead to God on their behalf? Here is a truth I hope will help. Everything Jesus asks us to do can be done *through the power of the indwelling Holy Spirit.* Do you remember what Paul said in Philippians 2:13? "For it is God who is at work in you, both to will and to work for His good pleasure." That promise encourages me, because God does it all; He works in me to do what He asks, and He helps me to be willing (when I'm not) to do what He asks—especially when the enemy is undeserving and the persecution intense—and it's all for His glory. Maturing believers know they must have the power of the Holy Spirit working in and through them.

This might be a good time for us to simply acknowledge to the Lord that we must have His power to accomplish this love-our-enemy-and-pray-for-our-persecutor thing. I'm willing, because I know that I cannot do it alone. Are you willing? You just might be surprised at what His power will do in you.

Maturing Believers Watch for Opportunities to Make a Statement

In this next habit of maturing believers, Jesus made a summary statement on how to deal with people who insult, or inconvenience, or disturb, or persecute. Our Lord followed the command "Love your enemies and pray for those who persecute you" with a *so that* clause:

> So that you may be sons of your Father who is in heaven; for He causes His sun to rise on the evil and the good, and sends rain on the righteous and the unrighteous. (Matthew 5:45)

Why do Christ-followers refuse to retaliate, to get even, and to get in the last word? Why do we respond to offense humbly, as if turning the other cheek? Why do we show patience when inconvenienced, and mercy when we'd rather seek justice? Why go out of our way to be gentle and longsuffering? Why do we refuse to hate, choosing instead to seek God's best for the souls of our enemies? Why all of these unearthly actions? Because we demonstrate to those without Christ how our heavenly Father treats His children! Maturing believers meet difficult people and difficult situations with grace, "so that" we may demonstrate, as sons and daughters of our heavenly Father, the character and nature of God. After all, simply loving those who love us is nothing.

> For if you love those who love you, what reward do you have? Do not even the tax collectors do the same? If you greet only your brothers, what more are you doing than others? Do not even the Gentiles do the same? (Matthew 5:46-47)

To the Jews, tax collectors were traitors. They worked for the occupying Roman government and were some of the least-appreciated people on the planet. (Know any groups like that?) Jesus said even tax collectors love those who love them back, and even Gentiles (referring to ungodly people) greet their own brothers. If we, as Christ's followers, treat only our fellow church members with grace, then we're no different from those who do not follow Christ. Once again, difficult people and difficult situations are our opportunities to live as God lives toward us. The apostle Peter challenged early Christians in the same way.

> You are a chosen race, a royal priesthood, a dedicated nation, God's own purchased, special people, that you may set forth the wonderful deeds and display the virtues and perfections

of Him Who called you out of darkness into His marvelous light.

Conduct yourselves properly (honorably, righteously) among the Gentiles, so that, although they may slander you as evildoers, yet they may by witnessing your good deeds come to glorify God in the day of inspection. (1 Peter 2: 9, 12 AMP)

What was Peter saying? Exactly why is it important to show, through difficult people and in difficult situations, that we are children of God? Are we just trying to be "better" than others, like some elite, religious uppity-ups? Are we drawing sanctimonious battle lines between believers and nonbelievers? No, never! As salt and light, we draw attention to the Lord Jesus, not to ourselves. We demonstrate His grace and His strength, not our own, so that others will be drawn to the goodness of our God and our Lord, Jesus Christ—and there's no better way than to love difficult people and to use difficult situations for His glory. After all, we too can be difficult people. If God can change us, He can certainly change others.

We end this chapter as we started, with Jesus' command recorded in Matthew 5:48: "Therefore you are to be perfect, as your heavenly Father is perfect." I hope that we now see "be perfect" with kingdom eyes, not as an impossible quest of self-effort, but as a process of growing and maturing by the Holy Spirit to live toward others as God lives toward us.

Perhaps my prayer can be yours too.

My dear Father, I understand my responsibility to live as salt and light. My eager desire is to make You famous every moment of my life. I sincerely want others to be drawn to You by my words and actions. Even in the face of difficult people and difficult situations, I long for people to see You.

I realize that my own strength is insufficient to accomplish this task, so I must have Your Helper, the Holy Spirit, to demonstrate Your grace through me. Father, live through me and love through me. Please use me to draw others to Yourself. I ask these things in Jesus' name. Amen.

Living It Out

1. What does living as salt and light actually look like in the daily life of a believer?

2. From chapter 7, list four habits of a maturing believer.

   1.

   2.

   3.

   4.

3. Loving those who love us is easy. But, as Jesus would, maturing believers love difficult people and respond with grace in difficult situations. Whom do you need God's help to love?

   Let's talk to the Lord about that.

Let's Pray

> *Father, please let every word I say and every move I make shine the spotlight on the Savior, so that the people I meet might come into a personal relationship with the Light of the world. I ask these things in the name of Jesus Christ. Amen.*

8

Disciplines of the Blessed Life: Why We Do What We Do

Matthew 6:1-18

Beware of practicing your righteousness before men to be noticed by them;
otherwise you have no reward with your Father who is in heaven.
—Matthew 6:1

Has it ever occurred to you that the Lord assumes you and I will serve Him? I mean actively serve as a lifestyle, whether in some organized act of charity or by various spontaneous, Spirit-led acts? Have you ever considered that He assumes we will pray, whether scheduled, on-bended-knee praying or instinctive pleas on behalf of another? Well, He does, and I can prove it.

Matthew 6:1 begins this way:"Beware of practicing your righteousness." In this setting, Jesus was teaching His disciples about motives of service. Notice that in His statement there was no command to practice righteousness, nor was there a survey asking if His disciples had given any thought to practicing righteousness. From His simple "Beware of practicing your righteousness," Jesus assumed every disciple would serve Him and every disciple would pray. It was just understood. Many (perhaps most) Christians, however, mistakenly believe that service is best left to a specially trained group of Christians, you know, missionaries and pastors and seminary professors and the like. Besides, church staff members are paid to serve! That lets the rest of us off the "practice righteousness" hook, right?

In their book *Great Commission Companies*, Steve Rundle and Tom Steffen expose the myth of a "spiritual-vocational hierarchy." They explain the fallout when Christians view "professional Christian workers" as the highest pinnacle and only conduit of Christian service.

> Professional Christian workers certainly have their place, and God does occasionally prompt people to switch vocations, but there is nothing vocation-specific about our call to be full-time bearers of good news . . .
>
> Our individual callings and gifts may differ, but mission [service] is nevertheless the central purpose of the entire body of Christ. The perceived distinction between "good" and "better" vocations has served only to undermine the effectiveness of the church because many Christians simply resign themselves to second-class status, or worse, become completely detached from any involvement in ministry. (2003, 12-13)

Wherever a Christ-follower is—the office, daycare, soccer game, or shopping mall—and *whatever* a Christ-follower is—a nurse, swim coach, parent, courtroom judge, or student—that place or vocation is the highest pinnacle of Christian service. God assumes that all of us, no matter our age, vocation, ability, or circle of influence, will practice righteousness.

As we walk through Matthew 6, let's explore some of the disciplines of the blessed life. But don't be misled by the word *discipline*, for these are anything but puritanical rules or starchy codes of conduct. No, those who dare to dip a toe in the rushing waters of Spirit-led living describe these activities as wildly terrifying—and utterly fulfilling!

The Applause of Men, the Ovation of God

It's indisputable: followers of Christ are to actively serve in order to display Christ and draw others to Him. Now, in Matthew 6:1, as if giving a divine essay entitled "Motivations of Service," Jesus began with this thesis statement:

> Beware of practicing your righteousness before men to be noticed by them; otherwise you have no reward with your Father who is in heaven.

In true fashion, Jesus panned away from outward acts of righteousness to focus in on the secret motivations of the heart. Why, exactly, do we do what we do? It seems we're motivated to serve, either

A. for a public show, self-glory, as outward religion, for the applause of men, or

B. for a private audience, God's glory, as inward worship, for a God-bestowed reward.

Motivation A, or Motivation B. We get to choose our motivation, our audience, and thereby our reward. In every word of Matthew 6:2-24, Jesus applied His thesis to the disciplines of giving, praying, and trusting. Let's begin with the joyous service of giving.

The Discipline of Giving

Pat Walker is in heaven now. That's one reason why I can give you his name. Pat was a very humble man, and if you can blush in heaven, then Pat is at this moment in full blush. He would want me to remain quiet about this particular act of giving.

As a family man, Pat was a loving husband, a devoted father, and a wonderful grandfather. In church, he was an ordained deacon and helped each Sunday morning in the Bible study office. In all things, Pat Walker exemplified Jesus' description of a giving servant. He did what he did to serve people but wanted no one to know what he had done.

In my mid-20's, I was Pat's pastor in Oklahoma City. Many young couples were coming into our church, and Pat Walker mentored several of the young men. One December Sunday, several of us "young guys" were standing around, discussing what we were going to buy our children for Christmas. One of the men casually mentioned that his children really wanted a swing set, but the family budget was tight, and there simply was no money for the swing set. The friendly conversation eventually ended, and the Sunday service got started.

Well, a few days later, the father who had mentioned wanting to buy a swing set called me. "Hey, Pastor, this is Gary. We've had an amazing thing happen. Do you remember last Sunday when we were talking about Christmas, and I mentioned the kids wanted a swing set, but the money was just not there?"

"I think I remember, Gary."

"Well, you're not going to believe it. This morning when I backed out of the garage to head for work, there were these big boxes in our front yard—with our name on every box. Pastor, it was a swing set, just like the kids wanted! It's all boxed up, and all I have to do is put it together."

Then with a chuckle in his voice, Gary said, "Maybe there really is a Santa Claus."

Gary and I both were amazed. We talked for a while longer, trying to figure out how that swing set came to be in his yard. After we hung up, I couldn't get this mysterious gift out of my mind. Then, as if a light bulb appeared over my head, I thought back on the men who stood in the group that Sunday discussing Christmas gifts for our children. When I remembered that Pat Walker was there, I thought, *It would be just like Pat to buy that swing set and have it delivered to Gary's front yard.* So, I made a phone call to Pat.

"Hey Pat, what are you doing?"

"Not much, Preacher. Just hanging around the house today."

"Pat, let me ask you a question. Have you been buying any swing sets lately?" The phone was suddenly silent, and for several seconds Pat said nothing.

Then the long silence broke with these urgent words: "Preacher, don't you tell anyone!" I laughed and promised to keep the secret, which I have kept, until now, knowing that Pat Walker is with the Lord.

Well, Gary and his family eventually moved from the state, and to this day, I don't know if they ever found out the secret of the swing set. Perhaps Gary will read this book, and "the cat will be out of the bag." And Pat? When he heard those children wanted a swing set, nothing on earth could have stopped him from buying that gift. He received no applause of men; but by and by, he received his most thrilling reward—an ovation from his heavenly Father.

> So when you give to the poor, do not sound a trumpet before you, as the hypocrites do in the synagogues and in the streets, so that they may be honored by men. Truly I say to you, they have their reward in full.
>
> But when you give to the poor, do not let your left hand know what your right hand is doing so that your giving will be in secret; and your Father who sees what is done in secret will reward you. (Matthew 6:2-4)

Apparently, in Jesus' day, some who were about to give to the poor first made a "public service announcement." The sound of a trumpet certainly would have drawn a lot of attention, as if to say, "See how religious *I* am! Notice *me*." These self-promoting givers chose their venues—"in the synagogues and in the streets"—and they chose their motive—"to be honored by men." They chose their audience (anyone who would look), and thereby they chose their reward—a few minutes of stardom on the silver screen of men. Because they did not give to an audience of One, the King Eternal who knew their hearts, Jesus called them "hypocrites," and He publicly announced their eternal reward—zip, zilch, nada, nothing.

Now obviously, many acts of service will be seen by others. Church choirs and orchestras, deacons and elders, Bible study teachers and mission committees all serve publicly. The big question is, of course, what is the motive behind the service? Pat Walker gave, unseen by men, to a private audience of One, for God's glory, as inward worship, for a God-bestowed reward. It may be wildly terrifying, but let's choose today to dip our toes in the fulfilling, joyous, rushing waters of giving for God's glory. And, shhh. I won't tell.

The Discipline of Prayer

Once a month, Tulsa pastors of various denominations meet to pray. We meet at noon, but we don't eat, neither do we talk about our churches. We focus on praying for revival in America and sometimes for other areas of need. One man in this group always blesses me when he prays. That prayer is a vital part of his life is evident. He prays with a quiet spirit, yet he prays with confidence. He prays as if he's having a conversation with the Lord Jesus, seated right next to him in a chair.

Over the years, this dear friend has walked through difficult times. Some have been challenges in his church; others have been family related. Yet, he never appears to be angry or visibly stressed, and I've never heard him say an unkind word about any person causing him difficulty. He is a man who is calm and filled with the peace of the Lord. From his knees, he walks through life with the Prince of Peace.

When you pray, you are not to be like the hypocrites; for they love to stand and pray in the synagogues and on the street corners so that they may be seen by men. Truly I say to you, they have their reward in full.

But you, when you pray, go into your inner room, close your door and pray to your Father who is in secret, and your Father who sees what is done in secret will reward you. And when you are praying, do not use meaningless repetition as the Gentiles do, for they suppose that they will be heard for their many words.

So do not be like them; for your Father knows what you need before you ask Him. (Matthew 6:5-8)

Here again, Jesus called out wrong motives of service, this time relating to prayer (and to fasting; see Matthew 6:16-18). It seems that the hypocrites paraded their prayers in public to appear impressive, and the Gentiles prayed loud and long to sound spectacular. These performances had nothing to do with God but everything to do with the shallow pursuit of self-aggrandizement. "But you, when you pray," Jesus said, do the exact opposite.

I hear Jesus telling us to exchange the filthy rags of appearances for the riches of God's presence and go to a private place (wherever that private place may be) to do business with the Lord. There awaits our Father who says, "My child, what can I take off your back today and carry for you?" The Lord will meet you and me in this place of quiet, humble service, for He "sees what is done in secret," and He will reward our service. The reward? Nothing less than the presence of God Himself and all that He is—the power behind the created universe, the healing Balm of Gilead, the very capable bearer of burdens. Who would want anything less!

On his knees daily, my pastor friend declares his own dependence upon God. He has walked through many of life's challenges, calmly and even triumphantly, with the Prince of Peace. Let us also run to our prayer closet and hit our knees. God awaits us there. And remember to shut the door.

The Prayer of a Disciple

Once we've shut ourselves in a private place with God and we want to avoid prayers of "meaningless repetition," how exactly do we pray? Let's survey Matthew 6:9-13, where our Lord outlined for us, "Pray, then, in this way."

Our Father Who Is in Heaven

With these words, Jesus gave His disciples the disposition of prayer: a beloved child speaking face to face, heart to heart, with his or her heavenly Father. He is, however, not just any father. We know that earthly fathers come in a variety of temperaments. Some good, some not so much. Yours may have been the latter; if so, my own father's heart asks you to consider setting aside that painful paradigm to ponder the truth that, in prayer, we approach a *good*, heavenly Father. Many in the Old Testament and in the New, and many today, boast on the goodness of God.

> Good and upright is the Lord. (Psalm 25:8)
>
> O taste and see that the Lord is good; the earth is full of the lovingkindness of the Lord. (Psalm 34:8)
>
> Give thanks to the Lord, for He is good. (Psalm 136:1)
>
> The Lord is good, a stronghold in the day of trouble. (Nahum 1:7)

Speaking face to face also means that God is, well, real. In one of those mysterious paradoxes, God is both unseen and ultimate reality. So, in prayer, God must be more to us than a divine concept. He must be more than a nebulous being we talk about in church. Christ-followers enter into prayer by speaking to a definite "our Father."

Hallowed Be Your Name

Now this is exciting stuff. *Hallowed* means "to regard as holy" or "to hold in reverence," and *Your name* encompasses all of the attributes of God. We are to regard all that God is as holy, and in doing so, we will be holding a right conception of God. In other words, our beliefs about God must be exactly as He is, nothing less.

So, who is God, and how do we conceive of Him rightly? Well, we can know this: because all of God is holy, then He (thankfully) isn't like us. A. W. Tozer said, "A god begotten in the shadows of a fallen heart will quite naturally be no true likeness of the true God" (1961, 3). We must not conceive of God as being in our image, because if we do, then we grasp in prayer for the help of a being who is no greater than ourselves. What then—when we think of God, or hear His name, or pray to Him—should our idea of God be? Well, the *all-ness* of God is infinite and incomprehensible, but He has revealed in the Bible *some* of His divine attributes. Keep in mind that He is all of these things at once, never only one to the exclusion of any other. For example, we learn in the Bible the following attributes of God:

✦ the wise God	✦ the good God
✦ the gracious God	✦ the self-sufficient God
✦ the longsuffering God	✦ the faithful God
✦ the immutable God	✦ the loving God
(He never changes)	✦ the merciful God
✦ the just God	✦ the righteous God

Because God has revealed Himself to us throughout history, we can know who He is (referencing the list above). We see that His character and His ways are trustworthy; so, in prayer, we can confidently entrust our needs and concerns into His capable hands. That, by the way, is the essence of faith. Prayer, my friends, is not really about our needs and us. Prayer is about God! In fact, our highest concern in prayer is God's glory, that we glorify His name. Yes, it's true that He's interested in hearing our concerns and in meeting our needs, but as we speak to Him about our needs and concerns, we do so fully recognizing to whom it is we speak.

As we enter our private place of prayer, let's remember accurately who our heavenly Father is. Let's remember that He alone is worthy of our trust. Let's remember to thank Him for being to us all that we need. Most significant of all, let's glorify and hold His holy name in highest regard.

Your Kingdom Come. Your Will Be Done, On Earth As It Is in Heaven

In every kingdom, only one can sit on the royal throne; everyone else bows to the one who reigns from that throne. In God's created universe, only one reigns supreme—King Jesus. The question is, do we bow to the reign of King Jesus?

Christ's followers who proclaim "Your kingdom come," boldly embrace their place as surrendered subjects in God's kingdom. As such, we desire His will to be done—in us, through us, and around us. (Why? Because we know who God is and that, in all things, He is worthy of our trust.) What is being done in heaven? God's will, pure and perfect, is being done in heaven. In heaven, all say, "Holy, holy, holy, is the Lord God, the Almighty" (Revelation 4:8). Not so here on earth. Sin's destruction is pervasive and entrenched. To ask for God's will to be done on earth is to invite God to bring back into order all-things-messed-up-by-sin since the garden of Eden (Genesis 3). We pray that all people and all of creation cry out the same worship to our eternal King.

What needs and concerns do you need to speak about to our Father? Ask whatever you will of Him, and then follow your asking with, "Yet not as I will, but as You will. Father, no matter how You answer this prayer, glorify Your name in my life and in this situation. Your name and fame is the desire of my heart. In all things, Your will, Your glory, and Your kingdom."

Give Us This Day Our Daily Bread

From our secret place, we lay before God our needs. "Daily bread" is not just the food we need for the day, but everything we need in life—physical shelter and clothing, mental stability, emotional control, the ability to relate to people. From the simplest needs to the greatest, we look first to God.

Spiritually, Jesus is the Bread of Life, our most vital sustenance (see John 6:31-41). King David understood this. Surrounded by a host of wicked enemies intent on waging war against him, David implored God not for a battalion of warriors to defend him, but for "You, Your face (Your presence), Lord, will I seek, inquire for, and require of necessity and on the authority of Your Word" (Psalm 27:8 AMP). Our prayer, like David's, is, "Father, if I don't have You today, I will not make it. If You are not involved in every part of my life, I perish." Do we seek for and require God's presence as our most vital daily need?

And Forgive Us Our Debts, As We Also Have Forgiven Our Debtors

Notice Jesus prayed, "As we also have forgiven our debtors." The forgiving of our debtors has already happened; it's in the past. In other words, before we ever start praying, forgiveness of those who are our debtors must have already taken place. No doubt, this is a challenging process. Not only does it require us to forgive but this discipline also causes us to pause and evaluate our interpersonal relationships before we move on in prayer. To do this, we must make a review of recent days and activities by asking ourselves, *Is there anyone I need to forgive?*

And Do Not Lead Us into Temptation, But Deliver Us from Evil

Next, the Lord related to us the need to walk through every day in purity. By instructing us to pray "but deliver us from evil," Jesus warned us that evil is everywhere, every day. We don't have to look far or long to find it. If we simply let our life take its course, neglecting to watch where we walk and how we live, we will soon find ourselves in the middle of evil. In this way, we must perpetually evaluate and monitor our surroundings, our relationships, and our thoughts. And so we pray, "Lord, keep moving me away from evil, and steer my life toward purity."

The apostle Paul warned the Corinthian church about such things, imploring believers to "Let him who thinks he stands take heed lest he fall. No temptation has overtaken you but such as is common to man; and God is faithful, who will not allow you to be tempted beyond what you are able, but with the temptation will provide the way of escape, that you may be able to endure it. Therefore, my beloved, flee" (1 Corinthians 10:12-14). Temptations do come, yet God is faithful to show us the escape route, a path we will choose only when we lead a disciplined life. "Lord, deliver us from evil—every moment, every day."

For Yours Is the Kingdom and the Power and the Glory Forever

As the Lord concluded this model prayer, He seemed to give us a summary statement. Prayer begins by remembering that our Father is in heaven and that everything about Him is holy. The Lord challenged us to ask Him for our daily needs and to forgive those who have wronged us, just as we have been forgiven. He reminded us that He wants to lead us into righteousness and away from evil.

Incorporating all these, Jesus said to remember as we pray that His kingdom is a kingdom of power and glory, and that our King is a king of power and of glory. In light of all our needs, highest of all is His kingdom, His power, and His glory. As we follow Him, we live in that power and enjoy His glory. What a wonderful way to walk through life, and what a wonderful way to walk through the storms that come our way.

If you take only one principle from this book to help you through life's storms, I hope it is the discipline of prayer. All difficulties in life can be faced on our knees, with our ears toward heaven and a desire for God's glory in all things. Okay, my friend, are you ready to pray?

The Discipline of Forgiveness

One of the most challenging disciplines of the Christian life is forgiveness. In fact, the very word *forgiveness* may dredge up distressingly painful memories of events or people we'd give anything to forget. With God as our witness, we really do *want* to forgive, but that person caused us great harm. Someone's intentional (or unintentional) act haunts us, the grievous words replay in our minds like a scratched record, and the offense seems embedded within our souls, giving us no hope of release. The fact remains, however, that Jesus said,

> For if you forgive others for their transgressions, your heavenly Father will also forgive you. But if you do not forgive others, then your Father will not forgive your transgressions. (Matthew 6:14-15)

"But Jesus," we say, "You don't know what that jerk did to me! I'll *never* be able to forgive. Never!" My friend, Jesus does know, and what's more, He also understands—for He too suffered greatly at the hands of wicked people. (Read Matthew 26 and 27, and then take comfort in Hebrew 4:13-16.) Yes, the offending sin is documented. It happened. The words were egregious and the act indefensible. No one is diminishing the deep and severe harm done. Yet, read this slowly—Jesus' words are right and true, and it is only in His words that we will find release from the resulting burdens that keep us bowed down. How could Jesus command such a seemingly impossible thing? Because He knows that forgiveness is best for *us*—physically, spiritually, mentally, relationally, and emotionally. Just how long will we continue shoving down the pain, when Jesus bids us, "Come to Me, all who are weary and heavy-laden, and I will give you rest" (Matthew 11:28)? Forgiveness is for our benefit.

What's more, whether over time or instantly, God can heal our pain. Many times, King David spoke of the healing and grace he received from God.

> O Lord my God, I cried to You and You have healed me. (Psalm 30:2 AMP)

> He heals the brokenhearted and binds up their wounds [curing their pains and their sorrows]. (Psalm 147:3 AMP)

> You have turned my mourning into dancing for me; You have put off my sackcloth and girded me with gladness. (Psalm 30:11 AMP)

We can take comfort and find courage in David's experiences, because, as we've learned, what seems impossible to us is completely possible with God (see Matthew 19:26). If we dare accept that Jesus' words are vital for *our* well-being, and they are, then the question is how do we possibly forgive such an offense? Stay with me as, together, we summon the courage to confront this most difficult topic.

The MacArthur New Testament Commentary (1985, 397) says the word *forgive* means "to hurl away." This word communicates an intense, forceful action. The idea is that when we forgive, we hurl someone's sin away from us. The action is planned; it's decided on and arranged in advance. An offense occurred and is acknowledged; it is then forcibly hurled away—so that it no longer has an effect on us. The word forgive also carries the idea of releasing someone from a debt—*someone who does not deserve to be released*, after all, that someone stole something from us! We may have lost one or more of the following:

- ✦ sense of security
- ✦ job
- ✦ retirement
- ✦ spouse
- ✦ children
- ✦ home
- ✦ reputation
- ✦ innocence

The loss is real and devastating, and that person owes us! Whatever happened, it was absolutely his or her fault, and no one on earth would blame us for holding that person guilty for the rest of our lives. But, Jesus said we cannot. For our own sakes, we must hurl the offense away. We must cancel the debt. Remember the prayer we just prayed? "And forgive us our debts, as we also have forgiven our debtors."

"Fine," we begrudgingly say. "I'll forgive. But I will *not* forget!" Forgiveness, however, does not necessarily imply that we forget the sin or hurt someone has caused. Instead, forgiveness means that when we do remember the offense, it no longer matters—because the debt is canceled, the person no longer owes us, and in releasing the offender, we too have been released. The scar may remain because all sin leaves a scar; but over time, it becomes only a reminder of God's grace that helped us hurl away the sin committed and release the debt owed.

What if we choose not to forgive? Well, it's simple. If we choose not to forgive, according to verse 15, we *interrupt* our relationship with our Father. Let's use me as an example.

Years ago, a member of a church I served complained about everything (we'll call him Smitty). When Smitty stood to speak in a meeting, all heads in the room would drop in silent dread because everyone knew the meeting was about to become very uncomfortable. Many Mondays, my assistant would bring me a note placed by Smitty in an offering plate. His cutting words were designed to hurt me and other staff members. And, nearly every month, I received a long letter from Smitty, letting me know all the things that I, as the pastor, had said and done wrong that month.

I found myself angry enough that when I received his notes and letters, I would pick up the phone and call him. On the phone, I would speak to him just as he had to me, bitter and hurtful. I even kept files of his notes and letters. Just looking at those files angered me. I wrote sermons pointed right at Smitty (although I never called his name—not saying I didn't want to), hoping to make a public example of his bad behavior.

Then one day in my quiet time, the Lord showed me that bitterness and unforgiveness were holding *me* in bondage. He allowed my heart to break over my own sin and pride. I felt totally out of fellowship with the Lord (see Psalm 66:18). One of the most difficult days in my life was going to Smitty to confess my anger toward him and to ask for his forgiveness. I then tore up all the files I'd been keeping on him. In doing so, I canceled the debt Smitty owed me for stealing my reputation and the peace and unity of the church. I chose to release Smitty, and in the process, my own soul was freed.

I wish I could report that Smitty's hurtful behavior changed, but it didn't. How wonderful it would have been if he had asked for my forgiveness and the forgiveness of the church, but that also never happened. As far as I know, Smitty never changed. But by God's grace, I did. The Lord helped me become a person of forgiveness.

As Christians, we are building our lives on the fact that we are forgiven. Our eternal destiny is determined not because we deserve it, but because God freely forgave us through Jesus Christ. We like that kind of forgiveness, don't we? How then can we continue holding someone in our debt when God released us from ours? It can't be grace and forgiveness for us, but justice and debtor's prison for our offenders. We must extend the same grace and forgiveness that God has extended toward us.

I pray you've found the courage to consider forgiving those who have caused you great harm. Jesus' admonition to forgive is, after all, in your best interest—physically, spiritually, mentally, relationally, and emotionally.

We've covered many great truths in this chapter, from service to prayer to forgiveness. Though we called them "disciplines," we found them to be anything but puritanical rules or starchy codes of conduct. No, those who dare to dip a toe in the rushing waters of Spirit-led living describe these activities as wildly terrifying—and utterly fulfilling! My shoes are off. I'm in! Dare you join me?

Living It Out

1. Why do we do what we do? If only we could surgically open our hearts to expose what motivations are there! Certainly, God knows. "For the eyes of the LORD move to and fro throughout the earth that He may strongly support those whose heart is completely His" (2 Chronicles 16:9).

   By what motivations do you serve, pray, and forgive?

   Is it so that others can see and applaud you?

2. Knowing that God has fully forgiven and released you from your sin, are you holding someone in your debt for what they did to you?

3. Who in your life needs to experience your forgiveness?

Let's Pray

Father, my desire is to serve You simply because I'm Your child—and for no other reason. I want to have a giving heart to bless others. Please teach me to pray in the perfect way that Jesus taught His disciples. I ask these things in the name of Jesus Christ. Amen.

9

The Whereabouts of Our Treasures and Trust

Matthew 6:19-34

For this reason I say to you, do not be worried about your life.
—Matthew 6:25

C harles Boyd was the owner of a large, successful car dealership in Oklahoma City. Because he realized his financial blessings came from God, Charles loved to give, and his giving demonstrated his profound trust in the Lord. As surely as temptations roll in, Mr. Boyd could have "treasured his treasures," but he instead chose to keep his eyes on his Master and to focus his investments toward eternity.

Charles was also a man who faced a series of potentially crushing storms. One daughter suffered debilitating injuries in a car accident. Another daughter died at a young age. His own ill health threatened the potential of each new day. Nevertheless, this modern-day hero of faith never lost his trust and confidence in the God of the Bible. In the midst of many storms, Charles Boyd exemplified the triumph of trust.

My dear friends, Charles knew the location of both his treasures (in heaven) and his trust (in God). For us to depend on anything this side of heaven to take us safely through the storms of life—whether the storms are financial, physical, marital, or relational—is to foolishly build our house on sand. Charles Boyd could have trusted in his earthly treasures to deal with all of the storms that came his way, but as a wise man does, he instead trusted the One on whom he had built his life, Christ the Rock.

By studying Christ's Sermon on the Mount, we too are seeking to live wisely. So, rather than depending on our personal treasures or crossing our fingers, hoping that life stays intact in troubled times, we choose to confidently focus on the all-sufficient One, who faithfully meets our needs according to His perfect wisdom. That, my friend, is the meaning of the blessed life.

The remainder of Matthew 6, verses 19-34, could be entitled any of the following:

+ "A Study in Contrasts," or

+ "A Tale of Two Kingdoms," or

+ "Are You Nearsighted, or Farsighted?" or

+ "The GPS Coordinates of Treasures and Trust."

Jesus presented in these verses the two incompatible lifestyles that all believers must choose between: an earth-consumed lifestyle and a heaven-bound one. Where do we fix our eyes—on this earthly kingdom, or on the eternal King? In short, where are our treasures, and where is our trust?

A Proper View of Earth

Before we begin, let's recognize that there is nothing necessarily wrong with beauty, wealth, and possessions. After all, consider the beauty of nature and the starry skies, all created by God. At God's instruction, the Ark of the Covenant was overlaid with gold; the garments of the temple priests were made of fine linen; the New Jerusalem (heaven) is paved with gold and its foundation adorned with precious stones (Exodus 25-28; Revelation 21). Jesus warned us, however, about wrongly handling things of earth.

> Do not store up for yourselves treasures on earth, where moth and rust destroy, and where thieves break in and steal. (Matthew 6:19)

The phrase "Do not store up for yourselves treasures on earth" pictures the action of stacking up coins. Charles Dickens' greedy character Ebenezer Scrooge, stacking his coins by candlelight, may be a literary exaggeration, but to "store up" treasures is to, in some way, treasure our treasures. Jesus said to stay mindful that our earthly gathered treasures and possessions will one day perish. Moths eat material things. Rust corrodes what it touches. Thieves of various sorts steal, swindle, and rob. And when we die, we leave, well, everything. It's been said that when a local busybody asked a probate attorney how much money the richest man in town left when he died, the attorney replied, "All of it, madam. All of it." Jesus in part was warning of making things of earth our priority.

So how do we ensure that we rightly handle things of earth? We daily acknowledge the following:

1. *Jesus (not you or I) is the creator and owner of all things.*

   Everything was created through Him; nothing—not one thing!—came into being without Him. (John 1:3 *The Message*)

2. *All things exist for His glory (including all we are and all we possess).*

   For it was in Him that all things were created, in heaven and on earth, things seen and things unseen, whether thrones, dominions, rulers, or authorities; all things were created and exist through Him [by His service, intervention] and in and for Him. (Colossians 1:16 AMP)

3. *We belong to God, not to ourselves.*

   Do you not know that your body is a temple of the Holy Spirit who is in you, whom you have from God, and that you are not your own? For you have been bought with a price: therefore glorify God in your body. (1 Corinthians 6:19-20)

4.   *Therefore, we live not for ourselves, but for the Lord.*

He died for all, so that all those who live might live no longer
to and for themselves, but to and for Him Who died and was
raised again for their sake. (2 Corinthians 5:15 AMP)

For in Him we live and move and have our being. (Acts
17:28 AMP)

5.   *We are dependent on God for all things.*

And my God will supply all your needs according to His
riches in glory in Christ Jesus. (Philippians 4:19)

We handle earthly things purely by acknowledging that all things,
including our own things, belong not to us, but to our adoring Father—who
freely lends them to us for His glory and use. For these blessings, we express
to God our gratitude.

To help us maintain a proper view of earthly things, let's burn into
our hearts these five truths and commit into our minds the supporting
Scriptures—as we learn to live ever mindful of whose we are and of our
dependence on Him for all things.

Fixed on Eternity

But store up for yourselves treasures in heaven, where neither
moth nor rust destroys, and where thieves do not break in or
steal; for where your treasure is, there your heart will be also.
(Matthew 6:20-21)

By drawing a direct link between our hearts and what we treasure, Jesus
gave us the GPS coordinates to locate our priorities. Find the treasure, and
we find our heart. Find the stack, and we discover what's most important
to us. The reality is that stored-up stuff on earth is temporal and perishing.
Jesus said our greatest priority must be investing in treasures that are eternal
and imperishable. We will seek first either the best of earth for no eternal
gain, or the as-yet-unseen treasures of heaven for no eternal loss. Let's dare
to ask ourselves, *Am I storing up treasures in heaven? Am I pointing people to*

Jesus by my lifestyle? What can I do, today, that is of eternal value? How can I use my material possessions to invest in eternity?

In our self-examination, let's be careful lest we think that Jesus was talking here simply about money and materialism. Keeping the entire Sermon on the Mount in mind, we must apply His words more broadly and fearlessly examine any misaligned priorities we might have—any person or thing occupying the treasured focus of our hearts. Don't get me wrong, many activities, things, and people—our career, hobbies, and family—are healthy, important, and good. God expects us to be responsible stewards of these gifts. But in our daily interactions and activities, we are to be ever mindful of eternity.

Living triumphantly, Jesus said, is all about our focus. Beginning tomorrow morning, please join me in praying a prayer something like this:

> *Father, help me this day to see every person and activity with Your eyes. Please turn my focus away from the things of earth, and show me how to invest today in eternity. I want to treasure the things You treasure. I want all that I am, and all that I have, to point others to You. Amen.*

A Clear Eye Can See Forever

The eye is the lamp of the body; so then if your eye is clear, your whole body will be full of light. But if your eye is bad, your whole body will be full of darkness. If then the light that is in you is darkness, how great is the darkness! (Matthew 6:22-23)

In teaching us to seek first the yet-unseen things of heaven, Jesus painted another picture of a Christ-follower's journey on earth. Metaphorically, the "eye" Jesus spoke of in verse 22 has to do with our focus; the "body" refers to how we live our lives. Jesus was saying that where we fix our eyes, or our focus, will drive our daily activities.

Think of a coal miner, led through inky-black tunnels by the light radiating from his helmet. His eyes are clear, wide open, and singularly focused. He has only one end in view. That beam of light floods his entire existence and guides his every move. Similarly, we must train our eyes to be clearly focused on things of righteousness; then our whole body, or our daily life, will be "full of light," focused on the Lord and His will.

The next picture Jesus painted, in contrast to the one just described, is a sad one indeed. Conversely, to have a "bad" eye is to have damaged vision, or even to have "double vision"—a confused and fruitless existence with no determined focus. James the brother of Jesus described such a state this way: "For the one who wavers (hesitates, doubts) is like the billowing surge out at sea that is blown hither and thither and tossed by the wind. . . . For being as he is a man of two minds (hesitating, dubious, irresolute), he is unstable and unreliable and uncertain about everything he thinks, feels, decides" (James 1:6, 8 AMP).

Let's again imagine the coal miner, standing in the same inky-black tunnels, but this time, with no light whatsoever. Imagine just "how great is the darkness." Jesus' language may have been figurative—hearts, treasures, thieves, eyes, and lamps—but the condition and the choices are very real. A clear eye focused on eternity—that's my prayer for you and for me.

The "Or" Principle

We work hard at compartmentalizing our lives, don't we? We have a business life, a family life, a social life. *And*, somewhere down that line, we have a God-life. In other words, we live out of many compartments, each holding some level of our allegiance and focus.

Not so in God's economy. Jesus reminded us that we cannot serve two masters (and again, look beyond just money). Think of it this way. Ours is not an "and" life, but an "or" life.

> No one can serve two masters; for either he will hate the one and love the other, or he will be devoted to one and despise the other. You cannot serve God and wealth. (Matthew 6:24)

The formula is simple. It's A, *or* it's B. Slave to earthly masters, *or* servant of heaven's Master in all we do. Devoted to the dogged masters of earth, *or* to the One whose burden is light, as we move from one compartment to another. Here's the point. It's not a question of whether we give every compartment our best. Of course we do. The question is, are we serving

God in every compartment? For that matter, who owns our compartments? Where is our highest devotion? If our devotion lies wholly toward God, then we can be slaves to nothing. With God as our Master, all else falls into its appropriate lesser place.

Beware of the subtle temptation to think, *I can do it all! All my compartments are running like clockwork, thank you!*—because Jesus specified, "No one can." My friend, you and I are not the exceptions. "No one can serve two masters," let alone more than two! We cannot walk in two directions at the same time; neither can we serve two masters.

The Triumph of Trust

I have a friend who worries about everything. If the sun is shining, he worries we'll not get enough rain. If it's raining, he worries that his plants will die from root rot. If his favorite football team is winning by a wide margin, he worries the coach will leave in the starting team and they'll be hurt. But if the coach puts in the second-string players, my friend worries they'll lose the game. This guy worries about everything! If he's not worried about a certain thing, then he worries that he apparently doesn't care enough about whatever it is he's not worrying about.

What about you? Are you a worrier? Does that tyrant worry seem to control your life? Perhaps you've worried so much and for so long that it has simply become a normal part of your life. This may sound strange, but have you ever listened to worry? You might respond, "Pastor, worry doesn't *say* anything. After all, it's a silent emotion that affects our minds and attitudes, right?" No, my friend, worry says plenty, and it's in our best interest to understand exactly what it says.

Worry Says Our God Is Small

Perpetual worry is a terrible and relentless taskmaster. It enslaves our thoughts, drains our energy, and monopolizes our time—and, it can even hijack our actions. Worry usurps the throne from our heavenly King, which is reason enough for Jesus to forbid it.

> For this reason I say to you, do not be worried about your life, as
> to what you will eat or what you will drink; nor for your body, as
> to what you will put on. Is not life more than food, and the body
> more than clothing? Look at the birds of the air, that they do not
> sow, nor reap nor gather into barns, and yet your heavenly Father
> feeds them. Are you not worth much more than they?
>
> And who of you by being worried can add a single hour to
> his life? And why are you worried about clothing? Observe how
> the lilies of the field grow; they do not toil nor do they spin, yet I
> say to you that not even Solomon in all his glory clothed himself
> like one of these. But if God so clothes the grass of the field,
> which is alive today and tomorrow is thrown into the furnace,
> will He not much more clothe you? You of little faith!
>
> Do not worry then, saying, "What will we eat?" or "What
> will we drink?" or "What will we wear for clothing?" For the
> Gentiles eagerly seek all these things; for your heavenly Father
> knows that you need all these things. (Matthew 6:25-32)

The phrase "for this reason" takes us back to what Jesus had just taught: no one can serve two masters (v. 24). Remember the "Or" principle? Here's how it applies to worry: we are either slaves to the earthly taskmaster of worry, *or* we are trusting servants of our faithful God. It's A, *or* it's B.

"Do not be worried about your life," Jesus said. To "worry" is to be distracted. When we worry, our eyes are distracted from our heavenly Father. Certainly, there are very real situations that demand our serious focus and concern: a child with a brain tumor, or a spouse with an addiction, for example. Even so, we can walk through any difficulty with a sound and triumphant heart *when we fix our eyes on the source of our help.* The worrisome situation may still be there, but it no longer holds sway in our minds; it is neutralized; it no longer holds power over us. The blessed life is neither strangled, nor controlled, nor shut down by worry. Why? Because we can rest, knowing that our situation is in God's capable hands.

"Life" is the Greek word *psuche,* and it refers to all of life—our mental life, physical life, relational life, and emotional life. This seems an almost unattainable command, doesn't it? That is, *until* we remind ourselves of God's character, who He is—Provider, Protector, Shelter, Guide, and Keeper. He can feed us. He can clothe us. He can handle our children and our career.

God's provisions are not based on the health of the stock market. He is working out world events for His glory. Look at it this way. When a good reason to worry surfaces, we can choose whether we'll remember who God is and, in remembering, whether we'll trust Him in that situation. When a coalition of armies threatened to stop the Jews from rebuilding protective walls around Jerusalem, God's servant Nehemiah turned the builders' thoughts away from their enemies and toward courage in God: "When I saw their fear, I rose and spoke to the nobles, the officials, and the rest of the people: 'Do not be afraid of them; remember the Lord who is great and awesome'" (Nehemiah 4:14). Nehemiah remembered that God is bigger than any opposition, a truth repeated throughout Scripture and history.

If you've been one who lightly says, "Oh, worrying is just how I live. My mother was a worrier, so I'm a worrier. I come from a long line of worriers." Well, my friend, here's the sharp reality: for a Christian to worry is sin, for worry says our problematic situations are just too big for our small God to handle. Yikes! In summary, Jesus said, "For the Gentiles eagerly seek all these things; for your heavenly Father knows that you need all these things" (v. 32). *Gentiles* was Jesus' word for pagans or godless people. When we worry, we think no differently from those who don't believe in God. Jesus' definitive statement? "Your heavenly Father knows that you need all these things," so trust Him.

The next time trouble comes our way, let's rehearse Psalm 125:1: "Those who trust in, lean on, and confidently hope in the Lord are like Mount Zion, which cannot be moved but abides and stands fast forever" (AMP). The triumph of trust begins when we decide to believe that God is indeed strong and mighty to save.

Worry Betrays Our Witness

Try witnessing to someone about Christ while at the same time worrying about some physical, mental, or relational need. We say to those without Christ, "Come on, be a Christian . . . and, just as I do, you too can worry about your life falling apart. Become a Christian, and you won't sleep at night. You can live fearful of the worst." The world says back to us, "Great, that's exactly what I want."

Or, think of inviting a guest to a church that fusses and fights over the color of choir robes and sanctuary carpet. It's no wonder such a church has no new members, never baptizes new believers, and, in fact, flat-lines as a viable witness of Christ. The main thing (salvation through Jesus Christ) is no longer the main thing. "But if your eye is bad, your whole body will be full of darkness. If then the light that is in you is darkness, how great is the darkness!" (Matthew 6:23).

If we lose our focus only to worry or fuss, we are no different from the godless. It's a hard pill to swallow, but worry destroys our witness. That said, let's put worry in its proper place.

Worry Undone

As we continue to travel through these liberating verses, let's listen to what we are to do instead of worrying.

> But seek first His kingdom and His righteousness, and all these things will be added to you. So do not worry about tomorrow; for tomorrow will care for itself. Each day has enough trouble of its own. (Matthew 6:33-34)

Several years ago, I had the privilege of preaching at the Yoido Baptist Church in Seoul, South Korea. The people and the culture are inspiring. The Koreans understand respect, and one way they show it is by arranging people at a meal table by age and position in life. Even though it may take a few minutes to get everyone seated, it's very important to have everyone in the appropriate seat. Similarly, in the phrase "seek first," the word *first* means "chief place at the table." Picture a banquet table surrounded by many chairs. Placed at the head of the table is the seat of highest honor—and only one can occupy it. For followers of Christ, only God and the things of His kingdom are to take *the chief seat*. He is our highest need and our greatest authority. He is the King, deserving of our complete honor. Above all else, we intently seek first God's kingdom and His righteousness, and He supplies our needs.

"Okay, all that sounds nice," you say. "But, Pastor, how does this work, practically, in real time? When life works smoothly and especially when it doesn't, what can I do to keep God, people and possessions, and troubles in proper perspective?" Well, let's make some general observations of how King David, in triumph and in trouble (some self-imposed and some thrust upon him by others), managed to turn his focus to the bigness of God. What did he do?

1. *David cried out to God.*

    Hear my prayer, O Lord, give ear to my supplications! In Your faithfulness answer me, and in Your righteousness. (Psalm 143:1 AMP)

    Save me, O God, by Your name; judge and vindicate me by Your mighty strength and power. Hear my pleading and my prayer, O God; give ear to the words of my mouth. (Psalm 54:1-2 AMP)

2. *David poured out to God his complaint.*

    The enemy has pursued and persecuted my soul, he has crushed my life down to the ground; he has made me to dwell in dark places as those who have been long dead. Therefore is my spirit overwhelmed and faints within me. (Psalm 143:3-4 AMP)

    Strangers and insolent men are rising up against me, and violent men and ruthless ones seek and demand my life; they do not set God before them. (Psalm 54:3 AMP)

3. *David rehearsed his trust in God. Rather than looking at the situation, he intentionally looked up to remember God's bigness.*

    I remember the days of old; I meditate on all Your doings; I ponder the work of Your hands. (Psalm 143:5 AMP)

    Behold, God is my helper and ally; the Lord is my upholder. (Psalm 54:4 AMP)

    The salvation of the righteous is of the Lord; He is their Refuge and secure Stronghold in the time of trouble. And the Lord helps them and delivers them; He delivers them from the wicked and saves them, because they trust and take refuge in Him. (Psalm 37:39-40 AMP)

4.   *David longed for God's presence and confessed his desperate need for God.*

I spread forth my hands to You; my soul thirsts after You like a thirsty land for water. Answer me speedily, O Lord, for my spirit fails; hide not Your face from me, lest I become like those who go down into the pit. Cause me to hear Your loving-kindness in the morning, for on You do I lean and in You do I trust. (Psalm 143:6-8 AMP)

Show me Your ways, O Lord; teach me Your paths. Guide me in Your truth and faithfulness and teach me, for You are the God of my salvation; for You [You only and altogether] do I wait expectantly all the day long. (Psalm 25:4-5 AMP)

5.   *David thanked God for His help and again rehearsed his trust in God.*

Blessed be the Lord, because He has heard the voice of my supplications. The Lord is my Strength and my impenetrable Shield; my heart trusts in, relies on, and confidently leans on Him, and I am helped; therefore my heart greatly rejoices, and with my song will I praise Him. (Psalm 28:6-7 AMP)

David is only one of countless others in the Old and New Testaments who, though they faced perilous situations or temptations, found all they needed in God. Remember my businessman friend Charles Boyd? He too had challenging life experiences that could have caused many worries, but he was willing to trust God. For Charles, life was not God *and* self. Neither was it God's plans *and* my plans. It was simply trust in God and God alone.

What about you? Are you willing, in determined prayer, to move worry under the authority of our big God, and all of your life-compartments under His capable control? And do the same thing tomorrow and every day thereafter? Are you willing?

Living It Out

1. Do you store up earthly treasures without being rich toward God with all you possess: your time, money, witness, personality, family life, business life, and social life?

2. In what compartments of your life—school, family, work, church, hobby—is God allowed?

   How can you make Him the center of each compartment?

   Jesus said, "No one can serve two masters." May Joshua's declaration ring in your ears and mine: "Choose for yourselves today whom you will serve" (Joshua 24:15). Will you join him by saying, "As for me and my house, we will serve the LORD"?

3. Has worry moved in with you and settled down as if it belongs? From this chapter, list the things that worry says.

4. Are you ready to admit with me that worry is indeed a sin that deserves no part in our lives? Admitting this and trusting God today and every day hence will be life changing.

   In what ways would your life change if you focused on the bigness of God?

Let's Pray

Father, I place my trust and hope in You. My life belongs to You. Please help me to seek first Your kingdom and Your righteousness. Help me to truly understand that I serve a great and awesome God who is worthy of my trust. I ask these things in the name of Jesus Christ. Amen.

10

The Speck-Removing Ministry

Matthew 7:1-6

Do not judge so that you will not be judged.
For in the way you judge, you will be judged;
and by your standard of measure, it will be measured to you.
—Matthew 7:1-2

D oes your church have a speck-removing ministry? If you've
never heard of such a thing, then you're probably also
unfamiliar with its qualifications. Surprisingly, no college or seminary
degree is required. There is no supervised internship and no ordination
service. Yes, this unconventional ministry is, in fact, *only* for recovering
hypocrites. That is, for those who have sworn off the exceedingly
unlovely inclination to look at another person's character or actions with
disapproval, which is usually followed by cold-blooded, hard-hearted,
mean-spirited judgment! Are you a recovering hypocrite (essential for
living the blessed life)?

The religious leaders of Jesus' day ("Pharisees," they proudly called
themselves) put on a nice religious show. They looked good on the outside,
but inside, they were as mean as snakes. Jesus called them "whitewashed
tombs which on the outside appear beautiful, but inside they are full of dead
men's bones and all uncleanness" (Matthew 23:27). Are you a hypocrite?

Obviously, Jesus had no place in His ministry for sanctimonious, hypercritical, disapproving, uncharitable, legalistic, self-righteous folk. No, His disciples were as real as they come. Their qualifications? Something happened deep inside when they met Jesus. They came face to face with their own sinful nature and admitted their vulnerability to fall to temptation, and, by gosh, they found themselves to be something they never expected to be—humble. The pompous-stool was kicked out from under them, and thereafter, they felt blessed just to have been picked up from the dirt by Jesus, forgiven, and given the opportunity to recover. Are you interested in recovery for yourself?

The Blessing of Transformation

The apostle Paul also knew a thing or two about being in recovery. In his case, he was dramatically transformed from hypocrite extraordinaire to humble servant of Jesus Christ. He could be, in fact, the poster child of transformation. (His is the story you want to cling to when you fear someone is too far gone for Jesus to reach.) Talk about qualifications, Paul was educated in all the right schools and raised to be a perfect Pharisee. His rabid hatred for Christ-followers was so widely known, the high priest commissioned him to eradicate Christians from the face of the earth (see Acts 7-9).

And so, he tried, until Jesus stopped him cold. In one literally blinding moment, the Jesus whom Paul so hated appeared to him, face to face, and everything Paul had ever gained was lost. This Pharisee fell to the ground, humbled by Jesus' transforming presence. Whew, can you imagine such a moment? In one of the most dramatic conversions in Bible history, Paul "got up from the ground," dramatically commissioned by God not to serve a cause, but to serve a Savior. In his own words,

> Whatever former things I had that might have been gains to me, I have come to consider as one combined loss for Christ's sake. I count everything as loss compared to the possession of the priceless privilege (the overwhelming preciousness, the surpassing worth, and supreme advantage) of knowing Christ Jesus my Lord. (Philippians 3:7-8 AMP)

I want that type of transformation in my life, don't you? To see Christ as my greatest gain, to count all things of myself as inadequate, to want nothing less than for others to hold Christ as their greatest possession. With that work of God's transforming grace in us, there is no room left for petty, self-exalting judgment. None. Paul's story illustrates becoming "poor in spirit"; and with that, his journey into the blessed life began. Would you like to be transformed by Jesus? Let's listen in as Jesus taught us first how to kick the ugly habit of judging, and then how to humbly participate in the soul-building, selfless ministry of speck removing.

The Bad Thing About Judging

Years after that watershed moment in Paul's life, he reminded the fledgling Galatian church of the principles of sowing and reaping. "Whatever a man sows, this he will also reap" (Galatians 6:7). It's important to remember that this principle works in both the positives (things we all want more of) and in the negatives (things I'd rather do without). So, if we sow toward others X [fill in the blank: love, forgiveness, patience], then we *will* reap from others X [love, forgiveness, patience]. It's also true that if we sow [trouble, gossip, blame, criticism], then we *will* reap [trouble, gossip, blame, criticism] from others. That's the bad thing about judging. Jesus said it this way:

Do not judge so that you will not be judged. (Matthew 7:1)

The word *judge* is in itself an ugly word. It means "to separate," or "to condemn," or "to form or express an opinion that separates." Both Jesus and Paul were training the church how to act like the church, how brothers and sisters in the Lord are to act toward one another. When Jesus said, "Do not judge," He clearly forbade us from forming or expressing any opinion that causes physical, spiritual, or emotional separation among fellow Christians. We are to build one other up in our faith, not cause separation by our judgments.

The truth is, however, that we form and express opinions that separate as easily as we turn on a water faucet. For example, we condemn the organist for playing too loudly, so we give her "the look" in the hallway. We deem too short the sister's dress in the pew behind us, so we bypass shaking her hand in the meet-and-greet time. We disapprove of the preacher stepping on our toes in his sermon, so we withhold our tithe for three weeks straight. What if we broke the ugly, prideful habit of looking on another person's character or actions with disapproval? What if?

Well, it's bad enough to cause separation in the body of Christ, but it's especially painful to us when, after *we* cause separation in the family of God, we're the one from whom others separate. Jesus laid out the clear consequences.

> For in the way you judge, you will be judged; and by your
> standard of measure, it will be measured to you. (Matthew 7:2)

If we sow judgment, then we will reap judgment from others. If we sow a shovelful of negative comments, then a shovelful will come back our way. It's an inescapable law of the universe, and it's certainly not a God-pleasing, church-building way to live. To stop ourselves from judging requires vigilance and ears wide open to the Holy Spirit's censure.

Let's take this study on judging just one step further (and please, no judging the pastor if this section steps on toes).

Can God Trust Your Church?

What happens when God drops a person into your church or mine, say, someone living in sin? Doesn't matter the sin. If a sinner comes into your church or mine, can God trust us to treat that person as He would? Which begs the question, how did pure, sinless Jesus treat impure, messy sinners? Zaccheus, the thieving tax collector? The woman caught in the very act of adultery? Two-faced Simon Peter, who professed his love for Christ, and yet three times swore that he never knew Jesus, just to save his own skin?

Here's the cold, hard fact, and it should make us squirm. People with great sin can neither meet nor experience Jesus if we heap condemnation on them. People whose lives are falling apart from sin cannot be helped if we separate ourselves from them by our words or our actions (or our church walls). Our practice must be to never sow judgment so that God can use us, His church, to restore fallen, sin-sick people.

If God *cannot* trust us to handle sinners in the way He would, then two things happen. First, our churches become nothing more than "whitewashed tombs that on the outside appear beautiful, but inside they are full of dead men's bones and all uncleanness." Second, He'll drop that sinner into a church body He can trust, among people who feel blessed themselves just to have been forgiven—and they want the same for other sinners.

A Higher Way

So far, we've exposed that ugly, separating habit of hypocrites—judging. We've seen the blessing of honestly facing the desperate nature of our own sin, which transforms us into usable, humble servants of God. We've noted the perils of sowing and reaping—to us, to others, and to the unity of the church—as well as the joy of being a church (or a Christian) God can trust to strengthen and build up the body of Christ.

Now we get to a higher way—the speck-removing ministry, a healthy process by which *brothers and sisters in Christ encourage one other to move forward* in the Christian life. The "ends" of this ministry is building up the body of Christ; the "means" is removing specks from one another's eyes—*with great surgical care.* As our Lord intended, the first step is for all of us to develop *the practice* of noticing the seriousness of our own sin.

First, Notice the Log

To further make His point of the absurdity of judging another's behavior or character, Jesus contrasted the effect of a speck with that of a log.

> Why do you look at the speck that is in your brother's eye, but do not notice the log that is in your own eye? Or how can you say to your brother, "Let me take the speck out of your eye," and behold, the log is in your own eye? (Matthew 7:3-4)

A *speck* could be a stick or even something as small as a piece of wool or lint floating by. By contrast, *log* refers to a roofing beam. Any judgment found in our eye, whether a speck or a log, will blur our spiritual vision and hinder all progress. Because Jesus knows our human propensity to *look closely at* another's speck, He built into this process the following "humility clause," just to keep us from taking lightly our own sin: what's in our eye, by definition, is always a roofing beam. No lint for us. We get only beams. What's in another person's eye, however, will be only a speck of lint. Look at it this way. That which I see in your life is always smaller than that which God sees in mine. A potential speck remover's personal sin is a big deal to God. Certainly, our eye-beam is obvious to God and to others; Jesus said it must also be obvious to us. In fact, before we even contemplate another's speck, we must first *notice* the judgment-log blocking our own spiritual vision. "After all," Jesus asked, "how can you inspect that which is keeping your brother from moving forward, when you've not even discovered your own sin?"

We desire to be authentic, humble followers of Christ, don't we? Yet, ignoring even the subtlest of our sinful behaviors can block our effectiveness. How can we teach young people about integrity if even one of our own principles is inconsistent or dishonest? How can we as parents expect high moral standards in our children if our own character and conduct are less than righteous? As a father, I long to help my children avoid some of the difficulties I've experienced. As a pastor, I love the people of my church dearly, and I long for the youth of my church to walk with God. From time to time, I learn of a sin wreaking havoc in the life of a young person, and I want so badly to help that student—because I see his or her spiritual life coming to a halt. But before I can remove a speck in anyone's eye, I, Pastor Ted Kersh, must make certain my own eye is clear.

Here's a helpful start in the practice of noticing our own logs. King David, a man familiar with sin, asked all-knowing God to keep him aware of sin, so that David could have a clean heart and a clear eye.

> Search me, O God, and know my heart; try me and know my anxious thoughts; and see if there be any hurtful way in me, and lead me in the everlasting way. (Psalm 139:23-24)

This may be a difficult request to make, but there's no skipping this step. And, there's no reason to fear asking, because progress begins only when we courageously address our own sin. Will you pray as David prayed?

Second, Remove the Log

Hypocrisy is the claim of being one thing, yet one's actual behavior doesn't match the claim.

> You hypocrite, first take the log out of your own eye, and then you will see clearly to take the speck out of your brother's eye. (Matthew 7:5)

The word *hypocrisy* actually means "to playact." A hypocrite plays the part of a Christ-follower well, especially when in the presence of other Christians. But in reality, Christ-likeness is not the hypocrite's daily practice.

Why was Jesus so emphatic? "Take the log out, and do it now. Don't wait." It's obvious: anything in our eye hurts us! Why would we knowingly protect or harbor self-damaging sin? Don't know about you, but I want those logs gone. They've held me back long enough. Once again, we can look to King David for courage and help in removing our own logs. This prayer is sometimes called "The Contrite Sinner's Prayer for Pardon."

> Be gracious to me, O God, according to Your lovingkindness; according to the greatness of Your compassion blot out my transgressions.
>
> Wash me thoroughly from my iniquity and cleanse me from my sin. For I know my transgressions, and my sin is ever before me. Purify me with hyssop, and I shall be clean; wash me, and I shall be whiter than snow. (Psalm 51:1-3, 7)

Did you notice the humility by which David approached our loving, compassionate God? At this point in his life, David had learned the relief of coming clean with God, replacing the weighty burden of carrying hidden and hurtful sin. Ready to get rid of some logs?

The Golden Rule of Speck Removing

At the beginning of this section, we noted *why* we remove specks—to encourage one another to move forward in the Christian life. And, we noted *how* we remove specks—humbly, with a clear eye, and with great surgical care. There's no way to come out of steps one and two without having been completely humbled. Having emerged from the process ourselves, we can then see clearly to take the speck out of our brother's eye; and in doing so, we empathetically follow the Golden Rule: remove others' specks as we would have them remove ours—gently, lovingly, and patiently. There's no place in the speck-removing ministry for harshness, because one wrong move, and the speck-bearer could be further disabled.

James the brother of Jesus spoke to the heart behind speck removing: "Talk and act like a person expecting to be judged by the Rule that sets us free. For if you refuse to act kindly, you can hardly expect to be treated kindly. Kind mercy wins over harsh judgment every time" (James 2:12-13 *The Message*). Knowing my own sin, I want kind mercy, don't you? Let's see to it others get the same treatment as we hope we receive.

Of Dogs and Swine

Concluding this instruction on speck removing, Jesus issued to His disciples a most peculiar warning.

> Do not give what is holy to dogs, and do not throw your pearls before swine, or they will trample them under their feet, and turn and tear you to pieces. (Matthew 7:6)

If you or I discovered a rare, valuable gem, we would treasure it, wouldn't we? Jesus knew, however, that there would be those who hear His teachings but will not respond as if discovering rare pearls that add value to life on earth and for eternity. Sadly, many would prefer garbage in their lives, as would dogs or pigs, over that which can make their lives beautiful and valuable. Jesus clearly warned His disciples that many would reject His truths and, in fact, would mistreat them for merely speaking of His life-changing truths. (But don't despair; for these we pray, as Jesus instructed us in the next part of His sermon, Matthew 7:7–12.)

What about us? Rather than settling for ingredients in life that avail us nothing, let us welcome the invaluable truths of the Sermon on the Mount, which grow us into strong, faithful followers of Christ, ready for the storms of life.

Prayer is the womb out of which the speck-removing ministry flows, for recovering hypocrites depend on and cling to the wisdom and guidance of the Holy Spirit. So let's take a close look at prayer. Here we go! Pray, Pray, Pray!

Living It Out

1. Do you take on the role of judge toward others, while ignoring the self-damaging sins in your own life?

    Dear friend, what sins are you ignoring?

2. How did Jesus treat Zaccheus, Simon Peter, and the woman caught in adultery?

    Knowing your own sins, how would you want to be treated?

3. How would God treat a sinner in your church?

4. Remember that to live the blessed life, you must be a recovering hypocrite. If you're willing, the following prayer is a good start toward recovery.

Let's Pray
> *Father, open my eyes to see the logs present there. Please let Jesus' love shine through me to both sinners and saints. I ask these things in the name of Jesus Christ. Amen.*

11

Pray, Pray, Pray!

Matthew 7:7-12

Ask, and it will be given to you; seek, and you will find;
knock, and it will be opened to you.

—Matthew 7:7

Remember the first day of your freshman year in high school or college? I can remember my first day of college. Just a few months before, I had been a senior in high school and had the world by the tail. I thought I was large and in charge of life. I knew all the students, teachers, and the location of every classroom in my high school. We seniors were impressive, and those little high school freshmen feared us. I just *knew* that when I showed up at college, my career of being simply amazing would continue. Wrong!

When I arrived on campus, I was shocked to discover how little I actually knew. I was now in a school where I knew almost no one. I had no idea where to find my classrooms. The professors had no idea who I was and didn't care. What I did soon learn, however, was that each professor thought his or her course was the only one I attended, and each class's workload reflected that belief. Overwhelmed? I guess so! How would I ever be able to comprehend and learn, much less apply, all they were trying to teach me? Yes, in just one day, I too, became a fearful freshman.

Life can sometimes be overwhelming, even for Christians. But take heart; there is help for the overwhelmed, and it begins in Matthew 7:7-8.

Overwhelmed? Pray

I wonder what the disciples were thinking at this point in Jesus' sermon. Sitting at His feet, trying to take it all in, they must have been overwhelmed. On so many levels, His teachings on God's kingdom would radically change everything—their thoughts, their families, their way of doing business, the way they related to God. No part of their lives would be the same. Something about Jesus had made the disciples drop everything when He said, "Follow Me, and I will make you fishers of men"; but perhaps they were becoming increasingly aware that His teachings and His type of fishing went far beyond anything they could have imagined. What were these fishermen to do with all this information? How did all this talk about heart issues—spiritual poverty, mercy, purity, salt and light, forgiveness—fit with the political messiah they thought Jesus to be? It was all still a mystery to them; the puzzle pieces hadn't yet fit together (and wouldn't until after Jesus' death and resurrection). But for the moment, Jesus was asking a lot of them, and they were overwhelmed!

Like the disciples then, we today may also wonder, *How in the world will I ever understand, much less apply, all that Jesus taught?* Well, it seems to me that Jesus could see that the heads of His newly called disciples (and our heads) were spinning as He unfolded this radically new and different lifestyle; so He seemed to take a brief break from the sermon to answer our collective question, "How do we do all this?" His answer? In summary, "Pray, pray, pray!"

> Ask, and it will be given to you; seek, and you will find; knock, and it will be opened to you.
>
> For everyone who asks receives, and he who seeks finds, and to him who knocks it will be opened. (Matthew 7:7-8)

What Prayer Is Never

Lest we assign to Jesus' words a lifestyle He never intended, let's talk about what this prescription for the overwhelmed is not.

First, it does *not* suggest a weak, helpless, unsure cry to something or someone "out there" somewhere: "Hey, you! Did you hear me? I've been talking here for a while. Are you listening? Knock three times if you're there." No, never. Faith says we know exactly to whom we speak—to our heavenly Father who knows our needs and promises to meet those needs—and we know for sure at least a few things about His character—that He alone is perfectly holy, gracious, merciful, just, good, faithful, wise, trustworthy, and loving. We also know that He is willing to answer His children when they ask, but always and only in *His* highest way and in *His* perfect time.

Second, in spite of pop-religious thinking, prayer is *not* "name it, claim it, and receive it." This contortion of God's Word presumes upon God to think we know better than He how and when to answer our prayers. What Jesus is describing is far, far greater than these man-centered applications.

Prevailing Prayer

Do you remember Jesus teaching His followers the discipline of prayer (Matthew 6:9-13; see chapter 8 of this book)? Well, just minutes later, with the foundation of prayer laid, Jesus described (recorded in Matthew 7:7-8) a certain quality of prayer—prevailing prayer. Notice how Jesus ratcheted up the intensity of each word He used: ask leads to seek, seek leads to knock. Prevailing prayer is not a one-time event. The language of the New Testament literally reads, "Ask, and keep on asking. Seek, and keep on seeking. Knock and keep on knocking." E. M. Bounds described this quality of prayer as "an inwrought force, a faculty implanted and aroused by the Holy Spirit. Virtually, it is the intercession of the Spirit of God, in us" (Bounds 1990, 39). Under the unction of the Holy Spirit, prevailing prayer persists.

> Importunate praying never faints nor grows weary; it is never discouraged; it never yields to cowardice, but is buoyed up and sustained by a hope that knows no despair, and a faith which will not let go. Importunate praying has patience to wait and

strength to continue. It never prepares itself to quit praying, and declines to rise from its knees until an answer is received. (Bounds 1990, 44)

Knowing that these were the men chosen to take the good news of salvation to the ends of the earth, Jesus was giving His disciples, then and thereafter, a crash course in accomplishing all He had been teaching in the sermon that day. He told us to be salt and light, but how? By continually asking, and seeking, and knocking to become salt and light. The same for laying aside anger, judgment, worry, and hate. For the things that overwhelm us—and for other needs as well—ask, and keep on asking; seek, and keep on seeking; knock, and keep on knocking. Why? Because we ourselves will never have even one ounce of what it takes to be a disciple of Jesus Christ, taking His gospel to the neighbor next door, to the corner drugstore, and to the ends of the earth. Accomplishing anything for Christ requires the humility to ask God, who gives abundantly to His children.

There are a few sure reasons we may not receive from God that for which we ask.

1. *We simply fail to ask.*

    To *not* ask, seek, and knock is a guarantee to *not* receive, or find, or have the way opened. (James 4:2)

2. *We ask with wrong motives* (usually self-centered ones).

    "Not Your will, but my will be done." (James 4:3)

3. *We have "a low view of God"* (Tozer 1961, vii).

    We doubt that "all things are possible with God." (Mark 10:27)

4. *We cherish our sin.* (Psalm 66:18)

Brothers and sisters, I urge you to reach back to that as–yet–unanswered prayer, the one you've given up on. Do any of the four reasons listed above apply? If so, make it your determined purpose to ask and keep on asking; to align your motives with God's Word and will; to be confident in God's power, wisdom, and goodness; and to repent of any willful sin. Then, under the unction of the Holy Spirit, approach the throne of God boldly in prevailing prayer. Ask, and receive. Seek, and find. Knock, and watch the way open up.

The Benefits of Prayer

Have you ever wanted God to just sit next to you in a chair so you could talk through some issue together? Well, in a sense, He does; for example, in Isaiah 1:18, God calls us to sit down and talk with Him: "Come now, and let us reason together." That seems to be exactly what Jesus did as He continued to challenge us to ask, seek, and knock.

> Or what man is there among you, who, when his son asks for a loaf, will give him a stone? Or if he asks for a fish, he will not give him a snake, will he? (Matthew 7:9-10)

I cannot remember my sons or my daughter ever asking me for bread. They've asked me for hamburgers and pizza and to put some steaks on the grill, but never for a simple loaf of bread. To us, bread is a complement to a meal, not the only sustenance standing between life and death. If my children were to ask for bread, they would most likely be desperate. They would be looking for sustenance.

The people who listened to Jesus that day knew exactly what He was talking about—starving children. Jesus reasoned that if a starving son or daughter asked for bread, no loving parent would give that child a stone. How deceptive that would be! In the same way, our loving heavenly Father will never deceive us by giving us a stone instead of the physical sustenance for which we ask, seek, and knock. In fact, it's impossible for God to be anything other than pure and true in His dealings with us. He alone is the giver of good gifts, and nothing less.

What do you need today to sustain you physically or mentally? Is it bread, perhaps hope and encouragement? Once again, when we ask God to meet our needs, He will provide our sustenance. So go ahead, ask, seek, and knock, and keep on asking, and seeking, and knocking. And when He provides, remember to thank your true Father for sustaining you.

God also gives us spiritual nourishment when we pray. The example Jesus used is clear: "Or if he asks for a fish, he will not give him a snake, will he?" A snake or an eel would be an unclean thing for a Jew to eat and thus would be an act of disobedience. But no loving father, and certainly not our heavenly Father, would ever give his children anything that would harm them or their relationship with him. Instead, God blesses us with spiritual growth and a closer relationship with Him as we draw near in prayer. By the way, the same spiritual nourishment occurs when a church prays. A praying church is a growing church. In fact, if you want to find a church that is spiritually strong, find a church that prays corporately.

Jesus then offered one more encouragement to pray.

> If you then, being evil, know how to give good gifts to your
> children, how much more will your Father who is in heaven give
> what is good to those who ask Him! (Matthew 7:11)

Jesus' reasoning for us to pray is a "no-brainer," don't you agree? The adjective *good* can mean "beneficial," "to be desired," "virtuous," and "satisfying." If you and I, who are at the same time loving parents and sinful creatures, know how to give what benefits our children, how much more will our heavenly Father give to us what benefits us! But, we must ask. Asking is an act of humility that acknowledges our dependence on God for all things.

To avoid being overwhelmed by the Sermon on the Mount, and to instead gain the benefits of the blessed life, we must pray, pray, pray. As your pastor, let me pray for you right now.

> *Father, thank You that You always give beneficial gifts to Your children.*
> *Some reading this book are desperate to experience Your goodness today.*
> *I ask You, loving Father, to help them as they seek the wisdom and the*
> *abilities to handle the storms they're walking through. I ask You to open*
> *the doors that need to be opened as they seek to walk with You. Bring*
> *beneficial gifts as we seek to live the blessed life. I ask these things in the*
> *name of Jesus. Amen.*

The Golden Rule and Prayer

As we come to the end of these verses concerning prayer, Jesus threw in something that seems almost out of place.

> In everything, therefore, treat people the same way you want them to treat you, for this is the Law and the Prophets. (Matthew 7:12)

We sometimes call this verse the Golden Rule. Obviously, Jesus was speaking to people who were very concerned with fulfilling the Law of the Old Testament. They worked hard to follow every jot and tittle of every legalistic law and manmade regulation ever written, all the while, missing the highest point—loving others. So, Jesus once again redefined "pure religion." He said, "If you want to fulfill the Law and the Prophets, here's how you do it: treat others in the same way you want them to treat you." That's it. Nothing more, and nothing less.

How does this relate to prayer? The word *therefore* links the previous challenge to pray with our duty to love others enough to seek God's best for them as we pray. Which begs the question, do you and I pray for others the way we want them to pray for us? Over the years, I've been guilty of reflexively saying to a struggling someone, "I will pray for you!"—but then I walk away and don't. In trying to be a person of spiritual integrity, I've repented of that sin. It's now my habit to pray for and with that person, right where we stand, that very moment. What if we prayed for people the way we would want them to pray for us? What if on our way from Sunday school to the church auditorium we had to walk around various ones praying for brothers and sisters in the hallway? Beloved, when that happens, lives change and churches come alive.

I don't know about you, but I see no downside to praying. Jesus' reasoning makes perfect sense to me, and I'm ready to start asking, seeking, and knocking for my own needs and for those of others. What about you? I say pray, pray, pray. It's a no-brainer.

Living It Out

1. Prayer is not "a weak, helpless, unsure cry to something or someone 'out there' somewhere." When you pray, how do you conceive of God?

2. List several attributes of God that are especially meaningful to you.

   When you pray, how can you apply God's attributes to troublesome situations in your life?

   Do you trust God to answer when you pray? Do you trust that His answers are best?

3. What an overwhelming thought that the God of creation desires to talk with and teach us daily! The psalmist said it this way: "But know that the LORD has set apart the godly man for Himself; the LORD hears when I call to Him" (Psalm 4:3).

   List two or three things you need to discuss with your heavenly Father.

   Will you do that now?

✦ ✦ ✦

Let's Pray

> *Father, I'm willing to pray with and for others, so please help me to be aware of those opportunities. Lord, teach me to pray. I ask these things in the name of Jesus Christ. Amen.*

12

Are You in the Family?

Matthew 7:13-14

For the gate is small and the way is narrow that leads to life,
and there are few who find it.
—Matthew 7:14

Have you ever heard yourself say something when, even before the last syllable rolled off your tongue, you were already asking, *Why, oh why, did I just say that?* You might imagine that I, as a preacher for more than forty years, have had occasion for at least a few such experiences. My wife has one particular favorite that we'll call "The Last Supper Incident."

While serving communion one Sunday evening, I was reading from Mark 14. This solemn passage recounts the series of terrible events leading up to the crucifixion of Jesus—the plot to kill Him; the anointing ceremony that intimated His approaching death; the Last Passover with His disciples; the agony of Gethsemane; His betrayal by Judas, arrest, and hearing before His accusers; physical and verbal abuse; and finally, Peter's denial of Christ.

In the middle of this passage, we read of Jesus arranging to meet with His disciples in an upper room for that Last Passover supper before He would be crucified. Well, the particular version of the Bible I read from did not speak of "the upper room"; instead, it used the term "guest chamber." As my eyes read the words "guest chamber," you can just imagine that my mouth said that Jesus and His disciples went into the . . . "gas chamber." Jaws dropped (including mine), and stunned congregants stared in wide-eyed silence, fascinated to hear more.

Unlike Ted Kersh, Jesus never made a verbal slip. Every word He spoke was divinely uttered and under the unction of the Holy Spirit. Why then, in the middle of His epic Sermon on the Mount, would Jesus talk about wide and narrow gates, and destruction and life of all things?

> Enter by the narrow gate; for the gate is wide, and the way is broad that leads to destruction, and many are those who enter by it.
> For the gate is small, and the way is narrow that leads to life, and few are those who find it. (Matthew 7:13-14)

Well, His words were no accident, of course. Jesus used sharp language and images out of necessity to describe the only way to enter the kingdom of heaven, a way taken by few and missed by many. The entire history of God's redemption story is brilliantly distilled in these forty-eight perfect words of Jesus. Let's allow His words to grab our attention, for by our response to those words, our eternal destiny will be determined. You won't want to miss a single word of the most important message you'll ever hear.

Children Only

People's lives differ in countless ways. Some people live comfortably; others struggle to make ends meet; many own little to nothing in this world. Some (as I do) constantly fight the scales; others never have a problem with weight. Some suffer from a devastating illness, while others never even catch a cold. There are two things, however, that we *all* have in common. First, you and I—and every member of the human race—will some day draw breath one final time. Second, at that moment, each of us will enter eternity, for no one finishes life and goes into nothingness.

Every breath previous to our final, God will have been relentlessly and fervently pursuing us, calling us to enter the kingdom of heaven. In fact, the sum of every verse in the Bible, from Genesis 1 through Revelation 22, is God's call to humanity throughout the ages to choose the God-following way of life eternal at that final breath, *not* the God-forsaking way of adversity and eternal death.

As we've seen Him do many times, Jesus turned conventional thinking upside down when He gave the following requirement for entering God's eternal kingdom: for "as many as received Him, to them He gave the right to become children of God, even to those who believe in His name" (John 1:12). Eternal life with God requires that we be His, and because eternity lies in front of each of us, we must ask ourselves if we are children of God. Are we in the family?

The Broad Way to Destruction

Following Jesus through His Sermon on the Mount, we now hear Him speak in vivid terms of the two ways to eternity—one narrow, and one wide—and the consequences of each way.

> Enter through the narrow gate; for the gate is wide and the way
> is broad that leads to destruction, and there are many who enter
> through it. (Matthew 7:13)

Jesus said the wide gate is easy to enter. Nothing is required of those who walk through it. No change of heart is expected. The way is spacious; it's a popular route, and there's plenty of company. Overall, it's smooth sailing on the broad way, though it does have one significant disadvantage—it is a superhighway leading to destruction. The Greek word for *destruction* means "loss" or "ruin"—physical, spiritual, eternal ruin.

Who are the travelers on the broad way to destruction, and why would they take that road? Well, some find it's easier to just follow the crowd; you know, the line of least resistance. Others haven't heard that the broad way leads to eternal destruction. Or, maybe they've heard and simply don't care—they're willing to roll the dice on the eternity thing. Many are busy walking and, tragically, give no thought to eternity. These are not evil people; in fact, we know and like many of them. The helpful woman at the post office, the friendly man getting gas at the pump across from you, and the highly professional person who teaches your child in school. Anyone who loves children automatically earns a get-into-heaven-free pass, right?

Most people want to go to heaven; but either 1) they wrongly believe heaven is gained by personal merit—the good life they've lived entitles them, or certainly shouldn't keep them out, or 2) they sadly depend on something or someone other than Jesus Christ to get them there—money, philanthropy, connections, the right of passage via Christian parents, a denomination, gold-star attendance at church. Have you ever considered that every world religion outside of Christianity is "man-focused"? That is, they believe that one gains heaven, or a better life next time, or nirvana, or harmony by demonstrating virtuous moral behaviors, good deeds, self-discipline, ceremonial rituals to appease spirits, literal idol worship, spirit worship of ancestors or animals, or submission to a self-declared spiritual authority. Please hear this. *The Christian faith, quite to the contrary, is based not on man reaching for God, but on God reaching for man.*

Yes, God personally paved the path to eternal life by the life, death, and resurrection of His Son, Jesus Christ. God reached for us. Jesus confirmed that these other notions are *not* the way to God when He declared to all, "I am the way, and the truth, and the life; no one comes to the Father, but through Me" (John 14:6). The narrow gate to life is ours for the taking, but only through Jesus Christ.

The Narrow Way to Life

Jesus entreated us to enter by the narrow gate, which leads to life.

> Enter by the narrow gate . . . For the gate is small, and the way is
> narrow that leads to life, and few are those who find it. (Matthew
> 7:13-14)

Let's make some observations about the narrow gate. First, unlike the wide gate, this gate is *small*; and like a turnstile, one passes through it alone, leaving everything behind. Here's how the apostle Paul described himself entering the small gate, stripped of every earthly thing:

> But whatever things were gain to me, those things I have
> counted as loss for the sake of Christ. More than that, I count
> all things to be loss in view of the surpassing value of knowing

Christ Jesus my Lord, for whom I have suffered the loss of all things, and count them but rubbish in order that I may gain Christ. (Philippians 3:7-8)

Second, the way to the gate of life is *narrow*, interestingly, a word that can mean "a way of groaning." How does narrow relate to groaning?

He Himself bore our sins in His body on the cross, so that we might die to sin and live to righteousness; for by His wounds you were healed. (1 Peter 2:24)

Read that verse again, slowly. Let it sink in. That, my friend, is concisely the good news of our salvation through Jesus Christ. Because you and I, as sinners by nature, were doomed and separated from God by our sin, God sent His Son specifically to become sin and experience death for us—so that we could be reconciled to God eternally. Jesus certainly groaned on the cross under the terrible weight of humanity's sin, for He "did not come to be served, but to serve, and to give His life a ransom for many" (Matthew 20:28). You and I can now walk through this gate at no cost to us, for the high price of entrance has already been paid. Jesus paid it all.

Third, the advantage of the narrow way is of incalculable worth: it leads to blessings today and eternal life with God. Because God personally reached to us through His Son, Jesus Christ, *the only way* to God is through His marvelous gift, Jesus Christ. Jesus is the narrow gate! There is no other way.

[He] has saved us and called us with a holy calling, not according to our works, but according to His own purpose and grace which was granted us in Christ Jesus from all eternity, but now has been revealed by the appearing of our Savior Christ Jesus, who abolished death and brought life and immortality to light through the gospel. (2 Timothy 1:9-10)

For by grace you have been saved through faith; and that not of yourselves, it is the gift of God; not as a result of works, so that no one may boast. (Ephesians 2:8-9)

> Jesus said to her, "I am the resurrection and the life; he who believes in Me shall live even if he dies, and everyone who lives and believes in Me shall never die. Do you believe this?" She said to Him, "Yes, Lord; I have believed that You are the Christ, the Son of God, even He who comes into the world." (John 11:25-27)

"Do you believe this?" Jesus asked His friend Martha. Please read her reply again. I wonder, is that your reply to Jesus?

Fourth, the narrow way that leads to eternal life is *not* an easy way. Throughout this book, we've identified many of the very real difficulties that Christ's followers encounter—persecution; the struggles of spiritual poverty, forgiveness, and purity of heart; the expectations to reflect Christ in all our relationships; the nearly impossible tasks of praying for enemies, turning the other cheek, trusting God for all things, and expressing love rather than judgment. Yet, even these offer the blessing of living a life that glorifies God, of living with integrity and obedience to our amazing God.

The apostle Paul "suffered the loss of all things" to gain Christ. It seems to me that even if heaven weren't promised him, Paul would have gladly followed Christ, no matter the cost. His life proved it. For Christ, Paul was imprisoned, beaten, lashed, stoned, shipwrecked, often hungry and cold—and yet he could say, "I count all things to be loss in view of the surpassing value of knowing Christ Jesus my Lord." To him, knowing Jesus was reward enough. The narrow way is not described as a way of flower petals and singing cherubs, but it is the way of a life that glorifies God and gains Christ.

Finally, "few are those who find [the narrow way]." Why few? Well, for the reasons listed above, many take the easier path, even though its end is destruction. Walking the narrow way would require exiting from the broad way, but the broad way is so comfortable, so popular and easy, that most never even bother to consider another way, much less search for one. And, because no one falls into salvation accidentally, to "find" the narrow way indicates that a search has to be made. Only when we recognize that we are spiritually bankrupt and in need of a Savior (having become poor in spirit; see chapter 2), do we have the disposition of humility to search for Jesus Christ, the only Savior.

✦ ✦ ✦

So, the two paths have been clearly spelled out, and these unmistakably different ways lead in opposing directions. Jesus came to earth to personally extend God's invitation to all: "Enter through the narrow gate." Believing that Jesus is the only way, I've made my choice to exit the broad way, to enter through the small gate, to follow Jesus on the narrow path, and to live to glorify God by my life, until my final breath takes me into eternity with my Father.

Every one of us will enter eternity. Where will your final breath take you? The best and only choice seems so obvious. I ask you today, will you "refuse to pay attention to such a great salvation as is now offered to us, letting it drift past us forever?" (Hebrews 2:3 AMP). If you're unsure, accept Jesus' invitation. Settle your eternity right now.

> *God, on my own, I am a helpless, hopeless sinner, doomed to eternal destruction and separation from You.*
>
> *But today, I say to You, "Yes, Lord; I believe!" I believe that Your Son, Jesus, bore my sin in His body on the cross, He died in my place, and He rose from the dead so that I can have eternal life with You. I believe that Jesus is the only Way, the only Savior, and I receive Him today as my Savior.*
>
> *Thank you, Father, for giving me life. Today I give You mine, all of me. For the rest of my days, be glorified through my life. I ask these things in the name of Jesus. Amen.*

All the resources listed in "Pathways to Progress: Resources for Your Spiritual Journey" (at the end of this book) will help you walk and keep walking on the narrow path to life. Chapter 13, "Beware of False Prophets," gives invaluable advice in finding a Bible-teaching church and spiritually mature, healthy Christian friends, all necessary ingredients to finish this life strong.

Welcome, my brother or sister, to the path to life. Welcome to the family of God.

Living It Out

1. On which road are you traveling today, the broad way to destruction or the narrow way that leads to life?

    I can confidently say to you that this is the most important decision you will ever make—because eternity hangs on your answer.

    Jesus said, "I am the way, and the truth, and the life; no one comes to the Father, but through Me" (John 14:6). It doesn't get any clearer than this. The narrow gate is yours for the taking, through Jesus Christ!

2. If you're on the narrow way, relive the moment you stepped onto that way.

    If you're not on the narrow way, get there today.

Let's Pray

> *Father, I'm astonished to think that sinless Jesus became sin on my behalf so that I might become the righteousness of God in Him (2 Corinthians 5:21). What a story, what a God! I ask for Your help as I walk the narrow way. I pray these things in the name of Jesus Christ. Amen.*

13

Beware of False Prophets

Matthew 7:15-23

Beware of the false prophets, who come to you in sheep's clothing,
but inwardly are ravenous wolves.
—Matthew 7:15

Not long ago, I was talking with our congregation about the scriptural warning against false prophets. At the beginning of the sermon, we projected onto the front screen a series of photographs of popular Bible teachers. One by one, face by face, I asked, "Is this person a teacher of truth, or a false teacher?" The final photograph was of me, posted with these words: "WHAT ABOUT THIS GUY? IS HE A TEACHER OF TRUTH?"

We listen to teachers in just about every area of life, don't we? Motivational speakers, radio personalities, counselors, Sunday school teachers, public school teachers, sports coaches, television preachers, fitness instructors, business advisors, just to name a few. Have you ever wondered if the teachers you (or your children) listen to and follow after are teaching truth, according to the Bible? What about the authors of the books you read? Can you recognize if they are teachers of truth, whether the topic is politics, economics, or world religions?

Certainly, in the area of spiritual teaching, we have the Holy Spirit as our teacher. So why is this discussion important? Because we also listen to people whom God has gifted to teach, and if we take seriously Jesus' admonition to hear and obey *His* teachings (Matthew 7:24), then we must make certain that what we hear and apply are indeed *His* teachings. Most are legitimate teachers of truth and worthy of your trust. Certainly, I hope that I am. Nevertheless, my people must be equipped to discern for themselves if my sermons are scripturally true.

What about those in your life who speak on behalf of God? Flash their photographs onto the screen of your mind. Are they teachers of truth? It is possible to know, so let's begin by examining the essence of truth.

What Is Truth?

Do you know how employees of financial institutions learn to identify counterfeit money? They study *authentic* currency—its characteristics, its quality, its markings, the way it feels. Because they handle the real thing enough to know inside and out what is genuine, they can then detect what is a fake. In the same way, Christ-followers should be so well acquainted with our Savior and His teachings, through our own Bible study and prayer, that we are able to identify true and false teachers when we hear them.

Let's do a brief study of "truth." We want to know some of its characteristics, what it looks and sounds like, its qualities, and its markings. What exactly is truth and where can we find it?

> ✦   *God the Father is the true God.*
>
>   For there is none like You, and there is no God besides You. (2 Samuel 7:22)
>
>   O LORD, the God of Israel, there is no God like you in heaven above or earth beneath. (1 Kings 8:23)
>
> ✦   *God Himself is truth.*
>
>   Into Your hand I commit my spirit; You have ransomed me, O Lord, God of truth. (Psalm 31:5)
>
>   He who is blessed in the earth will be blessed by the God of truth; and he who swears in the earth will swear by the God of truth. (Isaiah 65:16)

+   *What God speaks is true and unchanging.* It's never relevant to only one certain time, but is eternal, reliable, and always the same.

In order that by two unchangeable things, in which it is impossible for God to lie. (Hebrews 6:18)

Sanctify them in the truth; Your word is truth. (John 17:17)

+   *Jesus is the embodiment of truth.*

And the Word became flesh, and dwelt among us, and we saw His glory, glory as of the only begotten from the Father, full of grace and truth. (John 1:14)

Jesus said to him, "I am the way, and the truth, and the life; no one comes to the Father but through Me." (John 14:6)

+   *What Jesus speaks is truth.*

For this I was born, and for this I have come into the world, to bear witness to the truth. Everyone who is of the truth hears My voice. (John 18:37)

+   *The Holy Spirit is the "Spirit of truth."*

I will ask the Father, and He will give you another Helper, that He may be with you forever; *that is* the Spirit of truth. (John 14:16-17)

It is the Spirit who testifies, because the Spirit is the truth. (1 John 5:6)

+   *God's Word is truth.*

The sum of Your word is truth, and every one of Your righteous ordinances is everlasting. (Psalm 119:160)

True teaching finds its source only in God the Father, Jesus Christ the Son, and the Holy Spirit. There is no other.

Think about this. The *first* verse of the Sermon on the Mount begins with "[Jesus] sat down." We noted earlier that in doing so, Jesus took the position of a teacher, and not just any teacher, but *the* Teacher. Now, fast-forward to the end of the Sermon. Like an end cap, the *last* verse of the Sermon says,

"[Jesus] was teaching them as one having authority, and not as their scribes." My friend, every word recorded from the first verse of Matthew 5 to the final verse of Matthew 7 was spoken in the divine authority of the Teacher of truth. Preachers and teachers come and go, the names and faces change. None is perfect, to be sure. Nevertheless, by becoming intimately familiar with the real thing—its characteristics, its quality, its markings, the way it feels—we will then be able to discern what is true and what is error. Jesus is the standard by whom we measure all other teachers.

Beware the False

Continuing His contrast of the broad way and the narrow way, Jesus made a most sobering statement.

> Beware of the false prophets, who come to you in sheep's clothing, but inwardly are ravenous wolves. (Matthew 7:15)

Regrettably, all that is taught in the spiritual arena is not truth because Satan works quite effectively from the platform of false teachers and false prophets. As a true Shepherd would, Jesus warned His flock that some would seek to dilute and undermine the truth of the gospel. His word *beware* was urgent and emphatic: "keep your mind engaged," "keep watching cautiously," "pay attention to," "be cautious about," "apply yourself to beware." As adversaries to the gospel, false teachers don't wait for people to come to them; they are ever on the prowl, seeking to destroy (John 10:10), to devour (1 Peter 5:8), or at least to distract from the authentic gospel. That's why lone believers (those outside of the encouragement and accountability of a Christian group or church family) and biblically ungrounded believers are at particular risk. Minus the fellowship of mature brothers and sisters in Christ, we become vulnerable targets of everything false, whether false teachers, prophets, philosophies, systems, doctrines, or worldviews.

Jesus then characterized the ways of false prophets as deceptive: "They come to you in sheep's clothing." That is, they consider themselves to be—and want you to consider them to be—harmless teachers of truth and authoritative purveyors of good. But they are neither. They may look the part, but inwardly they are "ravenous" wolves, frauds, and swindlers. A cursory survey of the Bible reveals many of the following damning rebukes and graphic descriptions of the nature and ways of false teachers:

+ blind guides

+ sensual seducers of unstable souls

+ slaves of corruption

+ daring and self-willed

+ greedy and unsatisfied

+ conceited, with no fear of God

+ entangled in the defilements of the world

+ exploit with false words

+ creep in unnoticed

+ indulge the corrupt desires of the flesh

+ forsake the right way to follow their own way

+ lack an understanding of the truth

+ seek unjust gain

+ cause division

+ promote immorality

+ advocate unsound doctrine

+ scatter rather than attend to the flock

+ feed themselves, not the flock

+ lead astray

+ speak arrogant words of vanity

+ despise authority

+ malign the way of truth

+ introduce destructive heresies

+ bring swift destruction upon themselves

Strong language indeed for whatever and whoever willfully tramples under foot the true gospel of Jesus Christ.

The characteristics and ways of false teachers listed above are evident, but what about the perhaps-not-so-evident teachings of those false teachers? What does false sound like? Would you agree that half of the truth is false (a favorite seduction from Satan's bag of deceit)? Twisted truth is false. A slight inclination toward error is false. Any teaching contrary to the Word of God is false. Treating God as a means, not the end, is false. Ever-shifting truth ("mosaic truth") is no truth at all. Humanism (my happiness is the ultimate reason for my being) is false. Mixing Christ with anything else is a false gospel. Whatever elevates man or thing above God is false. Whatever distracts from the true gospel is false. A hyperfocus that ignores the balance of the whole gospel is false. A teaching that is confusing, unsettling, or disturbing may well be false and must be examined under the microscope of God's Word.

What about some of the teaching prevalent on television? As we study the life of Christ, we notice that He asked one all-encompassing thing from those He taught—He asked for their very lives. But did Jesus ever ask for personal items, or money, or a "seed gift"? No. Many times, teachers ask for much more from us (including money) than they will ever give, so listen carefully to the message. We must ask (and keep asking) of every teacher and teaching: Is this truth, or is it error?

Here's another qualifying question. Would this teaching benefit the persecuted churches of the world—the unregistered churches of Cambodia, the secret house churches of China, Vietnam, and Myanmar? I've worked with some true shepherds of these churches, courageous men and women who boldly risk their lives every day for the cause of Christ. Let's get real. Would "seed gifts" or "healing oil" benefit these brothers and sisters?

Whether they possess one of the characteristics listed above or all of them, false teachers and false shepherds are indeed the antithesis of a true teacher or shepherd. It is little wonder that the harsh judgment of God awaits them.

True Shepherds and Teachers

If we go through every bullet point in the list above and determine, one by one, the polar opposite behavior or characteristics, we would then have a good picture of a true teacher and a true shepherd. The characteristics, qualities, and markings of light and darkness could not be more different. A. W. Tozer said that true teachers glorify God; they place Jesus Christ at the center of Christianity; they gain inspiration from the Holy Spirit in accord with the Scriptures; they lead the way in displacing self with the person of Christ; they deepen our love for fellow Christ-followers; and they promote righteousness and reject compromise (1979, 58-62). In contrast to false shepherds, true shepherds desire to pour their own lives into ours, not to take from us. They desire to give to and add to our lives. They long to build the character of Christ in us.

In letters written to his young, pastor-friend Timothy, the apostle
Paul gave the following rousing challenges to true shepherds as to how
they "ought to conduct [themselves] in the household of God, which
is the church of the living God, the pillar and support of the truth" (1
Timothy 3:15).

> Flee from these things, you man of God, and pursue righteousness,
> godliness, faith, love, perseverance, and gentleness. Fight the good
> fight of faith; take hold of the eternal life to which you were
> called, and you made the good confession in the presence of
> many witnesses. (1 Timothy 6:11-12)

> I solemnly charge you in the presence of God and of Christ
> Jesus . . . preach the word; be ready in season and out of season;
> reprove, rebuke, exhort, with great patience and instruction. Be
> sober in all things, endure hardship, do the work of an evangelist,
> fulfill your ministry. (2 Timothy 4:1-2, 5)

Find a shepherd or teacher who follows these exhortations of the
apostle Paul and you will find a true shepherd.

Become a Fruit Inspector

An alert mind and a sensitive ear to the Holy Spirit are necessary to
discern truth from error. Jesus also taught the practical skill of inspecting the
fruit of a teacher or shepherd. It's actually quite simple: without a doubt, the
fruit reveals the true nature of the tree.

> You will know [false prophets] by their fruits. Grapes are not
> gathered from thorn bushes nor figs from thistles, are they? Even
> so, every good tree bears good fruit; but the bad tree bears bad
> fruit. A good tree cannot produce bad fruit, nor can a bad tree
> produce good fruit. (Matthew 7:16-18)

That teachers of truth produce grapes and figs was Jesus' way of saying
the food they dispense is consistently nourishing; it benefits and builds
the spiritual health of their flocks. The fruit produced from Jesus' teaching

perfectly illustrates fruit that nourishes. For example, when we hear and obey the teachings of the Sermon on the Mount, we become humble in spirit. We protect our marriages. Our minds are peaceful rather than anxious and worried. We pray and love rather than judge and condemn. We keep the logs out of our own eye, and we treat people the way we would want to be treated. And, because we believe that Jesus Christ paid the debt for our sins by His death (instead of trusting in our own righteousness), we will enter by the narrow gate into the kingdom of God.

In the same way, the results of the power of the true gospel preached are evident. Souls are converted, minds are renewed, prodigals return to the foot of the cross, sin and self are renounced, broken lives are restored to health, marriages are brought back together, downcast souls are encouraged and prayed for, the hungry are fed, the sick and imprisoned are visited. Highest of all, the reputation of Jesus Christ is lifted up in the community and *He* becomes famous. And all of this emanating, not because congregants sat comfortably focused on a teacher, but because all matured, and radiated the truth they heard, transforming inwardly and visibly their businesses, families, and communities. Dear brothers and sisters, all of that sounds like grapes and figs to me. The teachings of the Sermon on Mount have the power to nourish, and the resulting fruits will be plentiful and good.

To the contrary, the output of false teachers consists of thorns and thistles, leaving hearers damaged and malnourished. Contrast good fruit with "Send me your 'seed gift,' and money will come your way!" or "Think positive thoughts and you'll sail through life like a gentle breeze." God forbid! Who benefits from such an empty gospel? Do hearers of such pabulum look more like Christ because of the message? Is anyone hungry for more of God as a result? Are souls filled to the brim with God and spilling over to others? What do you think, grapes and figs, or thorns and thistles? This same question applies to the character of every teacher compared with the character of Christ. Does the person who speaks on behalf of God also display the qualities that our Savior displayed—humility, love, grace, forgiveness, and care? What is the fruit of the message? What is the fruit of the messenger?

When contrasting error and truth, A. W. Tozer said, "A bit of healthy disbelief is sometimes as needful as faith to the welfare of our souls. It is no sin to doubt some things, but it may be fatal to believe everything. Faith never means gullibility" (1979, 63-64). When listening to someone teach, we have the mandate to consider, *If I believe and follow what this person is teaching, will I be more like Jesus? Will this teaching bring nutrition and strength to me, or will it be harmful, as if swallowing a thorn or a thistle?*

Dear Christ-follower, for your own spiritual health, get out your Bible and learn to distinguish between fruit that is holy and healing and that which is deceptive and damaging.

Listen to What Is Not Said

We know what sorts of things false prophets and teachers do and say. But what things do they *not* say that we should listen to? Jesus said, "A good tree cannot produce bad fruit, nor can a bad tree produce good fruit." In other words, there are some good things that bad trees (false teachers) simply cannot produce and cannot say. For example, some false teachers will not say that we are justified through grace alone, by faith alone, in Christ alone. Others will not acknowledge that Jesus is God's only Son, that salvation is found in no other, or that only the Bible is God's inspired Word. Many false teachers will not speak against willful sin in a Christian's life or denounce pharisaism in the church. They will not teach the whole gospel (because they don't believe it?); consequently, they cannot possibly glorify God by their words and life.

It's critically important not only to observe how teachers live but also to listen for what they do not say.

Depart from Me

If trees that consistently produce grapes and figs are good for nourishment, then what are trees that produce thorns and thistles good for? Jesus' straightforward answer? "Nothing!"

> Every tree that does not bear good fruit is cut down and thrown into the fire. So then, you will know them by their fruits.
>
> Not everyone who says to Me, "Lord, Lord," will enter the kingdom of heaven, but he who does the will of My Father who is in heaven will enter. Many will say to Me on that day, "Lord,

> Lord, did we not prophesy in Your name, and in Your name cast
> out demons, and in Your name perform many miracles?" And
> then I will declare to them, "I never knew you; depart from me,
> you who practice lawlessness." (Matthew 7:19-23)

Chilling words, aren't they? The bottom line is that there is only one true gospel and anything less is not. Because false prophets refuse the soul-transforming power of the Holy Spirit, their realm of operation can be only in untruth. They cannot say, as the apostle Paul said, "I have been crucified with Christ; and it is no longer I who live, but Christ lives in me," for they will not turn from sin and crucify their flesh—Christ simply does not live in them. They insist on being little kings in their own little kingdoms; and, thereby, they forfeit the hope of God's eternal kingdom. They have their reward. In the end, no matter how vehemently they protest and plead on the basis of their own self-efforts, the Savior who died for them must declare, "I never knew you; depart from Me." For heaven is gained not by outward appearances, but by inward transformation.

The blessed life is a life in which we must have teachers. Because truth comes only from true teachers, we must be vigilant and discerning. May I suggest five questions to ask when observing and listening to Bible teachers?

1. What do I know about their character and ways?

2. What are they feeding me?

3. What are they *not* saying?

4. Would this message benefit the persecuted church?

5. If I accept what they are teaching, will God receive the ultimate glory?

Dear brothers and sisters, wisdom says that it really does matter to what and to whom we listen, both inside and outside the church. I pray that you find wisdom in this chapter to guard your eyes, your ears, and your hearts. And carry out these challenges by our Lord with prayer and grace.

Let me warn you therefore, beloved, that knowing these things beforehand, you should be on your guard, lest you be carried away by the error of lawless and wicked persons and fall from your own present firm condition.

But grow in grace (undeserved favor, spiritual strength) and recognition and knowledge and understanding of our Lord and Savior Jesus Christ (the Messiah). To Him be glory (honor, majesty, and splendor) both now and to the day of eternity. Amen. (2 Peter 3:17–18 AMP)

Living It Out

1. Jesus' teaching concerning false teachers is serious, and we must listen.

   + False teachers come after you.

   + False teachers appear to be good shepherds.

   + False teachers look for what you can put into *their* lives.

   + False teachers may or may not have a thorny character.

   Do you heed Jesus' warning to "beware" of false teachers?

2. We can know if a teacher is proclaiming truth only when we know from the Bible who God is and how He acts. Are you a student of the Bible?

   As you listen to teachers and preachers, are you willing to ask yourself, "What am I being fed, what will be produced in my life if I listen, and does this teaching bring honor and glory to God and God alone?"

Let's Pray

> *Father, if I'm to live the blessed life, I must fill my heart and mind with the truth of Your Word. Please give me wisdom to discern the difference between a true teacher and a false teacher. I ask these things in the name of Jesus Christ. Amen.*

Afterword

Well, my brothers and sisters, we've come full circle. We end this guided tour right where we started, with the parable of the two builders.

> Therefore everyone who hears these words of Mine, and acts upon them, may be compared to a wise man, who built his house upon the rock.
>
> And the rain descended, and the floods came, and the winds blew, and burst against that house; and yet it did not fall, for it had been founded upon the rock. And everyone who hears these words of Mine, and does not act upon them, will be like a foolish man, who built his house upon the sand. And the rain descended, and the floods came, and the winds blew, and burst against that house; and it fell, and great was its fall. (Matthew 7:24-27)

Throughout the Sermon on the Mount, we've seen that wise builders build their lives on the teachings of Jesus Christ. We've seen *how* they build, and we've seen the blessed outcomes of careful building, both in this life and for eternity. With that, Matthew recorded the reaction of the crowd as Jesus spoke the final amen to His Sermon.

> When Jesus had finished these sayings [the Sermon on the Mount], the crowds were astonished and overwhelmed with bewildered wonder at His teaching. (Matthew 7:28 AMP)

The words of our Savior are still astonishing, and the blessed life lived by those who obey them is astonishingly fulfilling. The decision before us today is to build wisely or to not. It's that clear, and it's never too late to begin.

I pray, dear friends, that you choose to live blessed.

Pathways to Progress

Resources for
Your Spiritual Journey

Following Christ is not a one-time decision made and then forgotten. No, it's a step-by-step adventure that lasts a lifetime. If you've decided to anchor your life on the teachings of Jesus and you're wondering, *Where do I go from here?* then the resources found in this section will point the way. We call it "Pathways to Progress: Resources for Your Spiritual Journey." It begins with a brief look at the spiritual-growth habits of Bible study, prayer, and Christian service, followed by a well-built list of resources from some of Christianity's proven Bible teachers.

I'm asking the Lord to use these resources to help build your life, marriage, home, and witness on the solid foundation of Jesus Christ. So, get your walking shoes on, and let's get started!

Bible Study

There is absolutely no way to proceed in our spiritual journey without daily Bible study. In fact, let me say it more clearly. There is absolutely no way to proceed in our spiritual journey without *personal, private Bible study.*

While every Christian should be involved in a Bible study with other believers on Sunday or during the week, group Bible study is not where we gain our greatest growth. The most significant progress we'll make in our spiritual journey will come from time spent alone, every day, in God's Word.

Our souls grow weak and famished if we fail to feed daily on God's Word. The apostle Peter said it this way: "Like newborn babies, long for the pure milk of the word, so that by it you may grow in respect to salvation" (1 Peter 2:2). The "pure milk of the word" is the Word of God (the Bible) with nothing added to it. Sure, there are times when we need someone to help us understand the Bible, but deep, personal growth comes when the Holy Spirit speaks straight to our own heart in our own study of the Bible.

There are many ways to accomplish personal Bible study, because one size does not fit all. So allow yourself the freedom to find what practice works best for you. The key is consistency. The following is a simple approach that works for me:

1. *Begin with a brief prayer.* My prayer goes something like this: "Lord, You said in Your Word that the Holy Spirit is my teacher, so I ask the Holy Spirit to teach me as I read the Bible. Please give me ears to hear and eyes to see truth. Lord, I commit myself to apply Your Word to my life, so please show me how You want to change me. In Jesus' name I ask You. Amen."

2. *Read from the Psalms and Proverbs.*

    Considered "wisdom" literature, the Psalms and Proverbs supply much-needed help for each day. So, I like to read five chapters from the book of Psalms every day, a practice that allows me to read the entire book monthly; and I read one chapter from Proverbs every day, allowing me to read that book monthly.

3. *Read from a book of the Bible.*

    I have no set plan for which book of the Bible I read through, though I usually alternate between a book in the Old Testament and one in the New.

    Once I've chosen a book, I read for comfort, not with legalistic goals. In other words, I allow the Holy Spirit to guide me in how much I read. It may be a chapter or two, or several chapters. My desire is not to read for reading's sake nor to check Bible-reading off my task list, but to learn and to allow the Word of God to change me. Reading for comfort does this for me.

The important thing is to let the Word of God sink into your heart and mind; so don't let your desire to complete a book cause stress. The idea is to grow in the Lord.

When I read a New Testament epistle, I prefer reading all chapters in one setting; that helps me gain the context of that particular epistle.

4. *Keep a daily journal.*

As the Holy Spirit reveals truth during my study of the Bible, I write it down. For example, I may learn from Exodus 14 that God is the Protector and Deliverer of His people. So, I record in my journal that valuable, eternal truth and its scriptural basis; that way, I can remember it, meditate on it, pray about it, and reference it in the future.

Also, as I read, I'm always asking, "Lord, how do I live out that verse?" or, "How can I experience these truths in my life?" In whatever way the Holy Spirit applies that day's Bible reading to my life, I record that as well. Then, I refer to these journal notes during my prayer time. My journal is a collection of God communing with me.

Prayer

Just as reading the Bible daily is necessary to continue our spiritual journey, so is it important to pray every day and even throughout the day. In fact, the more we learn about God from the Bible, the more we will want to commune with Him.

If you're concerned that you don't know *how* to pray, just ask the Holy Spirit to teach you. Even the disciples asked Jesus to teach them how to pray (Luke 11:1-13). So, ask.

At the same time, never worry that your prayers aren't as "eloquent" as Mr. or Mrs. So-and-So's prayers, because prayer is simply communicating with your heavenly Father. He communicates with us through His Word and His Spirit, and we talk with Him through prayer. Be confident that God wants to commune with *you*.

The following are a few thoughts from my own prayer time that may give a little direction in the habit of prayer:

+ *Gain a clean heart, and then praise God.*

   Because the Bible says, "If I regard wickedness in my heart, the Lord will not hear" (Psalms 66:18), I begin my prayer time with confession. It's important for me to have my heart and life clean before the Lord as I pray.

   Following a time of confession, I enjoy praising the Lord, many times drawing from the Psalm that I read that day. Sometimes I read aloud or sing a Psalm, just as if I'm singing to the Lord. I even make up my own tunes! I praise the Lord for His goodness, His grace, and His glory. If you need a starter, read aloud Psalm 33, Psalm 107, or Psalm 138. As you praise God, He will bring to your mind other reasons to praise Him.

+ *Pray for people and situations.*

   During your Bible study time, the Holy Spirit probably brought to your mind specific people who need to know God, or people and situations needing God's help in some way, and you recorded those in your journal. Pray for them now as the Holy Spirit directs, and be watching for God to answer. His answer may or may not be *your* answer, but it will always be the perfect answer. When it comes, record God's answer in your journal, praise Him for it, and when your faith needs a boost, recall His faithfulness and goodness to hear and answer prayer.

   In 1 Timothy 2:1-3, we're told to pray for government officials and for others who lead us (including your pastor). I think it's good to take one day a week to pray for our president, our governor, and our legislators. This is also a good time to pray for missions and missionaries around the world.

+ *End by being still before the Lord.*

Communing with God (prayer) is not only a time when we talk to the Lord but it's also a time when He speaks to us (because we're still and quiet enough to listen!). So, I always take a few minutes to simply be still and quiet in order to hear from the Lord.

He may give me insight into the Scripture I read that day or allow me to see how He wants to change my life. So, I take the time to be quiet, to listen, and to record in my journal, for meditation and prayer, anything I sense Him saying to me in this most intimate of moments with my Savior.

Ministry and Christian Service

According to 1 Corinthians 12, every Christ-follower is endowed with distinctive gifts with which to serve the Lord in a distinctive way. God has given certain gifts to you and certain gifts to me, all of them empowered by the same Holy Spirit and for the glory of God.

As you study the Bible and pray every day, ask the Lord to guide you toward the ministry and service opportunities He has for you. Seek the counsel of your pastor and other spiritual leaders about places of ministry and service that fit the gifts God has given you. Your greatest fulfillment and fruitfulness will come when you serve in the name of Jesus and according to your particular gifts.

Additional Resources

www.blackaby.net

Find many excellent resources by Henry and Richard Blackaby, focused on helping people to experience God; helping people and churches to return to God (revival); helping church, business, and family leaders to move others onto God's agenda. Audio resources, books, daily devotionals, prayer room, curriculums, videos, online classes, leadership coaching and conferences, and much more. See a review of Richard Blackaby's book *Putting a Face on Grace* in the next section, "Recommended Books."

www.equippedbyhisword.org

Equipped By His Word is the non-profit ministry of Dr. Ted Kersh. Find resources to help in your spiritual journey: encouraging blog posts; practical, Bible-focused sermons and articles; and Book of the Month reviews (Ted says that "a growing Christian is a reading Christian"). Also, through conferences on church leadership and on the Christian life, Pastor Kersh equips churches and church leaders to fulfill their God-given mission.

www.frizzellministries.org

Gregory Frizzell Prayer and Renewal Ministries. Find deep, practical books used throughout the world to teach Christian leaders, churches, and individual believers on prayer and spiritual awakening. Topics include holiness, revival, prayer, evangelism, relationships, peace, and more.

www.hhbc.com

Deepen your understanding of God's Word as you worship online with gifted teacher Dennis Newkirk, pastor of Henderson Hills Baptist Church, Edmond, Oklahoma.

www.michaelcatt.com

Books, blogs, films, podcasts, and conferences. Inspiration defines the ministry of Michael Catt, senior pastor of Sherwood Baptist Church, Albany, Georgia, and founder of its film ministry, Sherwood Pictures, producer of *Facing the Giants, Fireproof,* and *Courageous.* See just a few of Michael's bold and encouraging books listed in the next section, "Recommended Books."

www.navigators.org

Navigators walk alongside Christ's followers on their spiritual journey, supporting them as they search the Word of God to chart the course of their lives. The hallmarks of this ministry are small-group studies and one-to-one relationships focused on discipleship. Navigators touches lives on college campuses, military bases, downtown offices, urban neighborhoods, prisons, and youth camps. Find books, articles, devotionals, service opportunities, and groups that meet in your area.

www.precept.org

Precept Ministries International exists to establish people in God's Word. The ministry trains millions of men, women, teens, and children around the world to discover God's truth for themselves, using the inductive Bible study method. Through this site, find an inductive Bible study, training workshop, or conference in your area.

www.tomelliff.com

Living in the Word Publications is the writing and speaking ministry of Dr. Tom Elliff. Drawing from his years of experience with the International Mission Board (first in spiritual nurture and church relations and now as president), Tom encourages believers in Bible truths and discipleship through his books, blogs, and conferences. See a review of *The Broken Curse* in the following section.

Recommended Books

These highly recommended, Bible-based, classics will strengthen and illuminate your spiritual journey. For each title, you'll find a general description of its topic (PRAYER, CHRISTIAN SERVICE, REFERENCE, BIBLE STUDY, DEVOTIONAL, CHRISTIAN LIVING, FOUNDATIONS, REVIVAL) as well as a brief review of the book.

No biographies are listed herein, but there are many Christian heroes of the faith whose lives display the splendor of God through the life of an obedient servant of Christ. For example, George Mueller, Billy Graham, Jim Elliott, Dwight L. Moody, John Newton, Fanny J. Crosby, William Wilberforce, Eric Liddell, David Brainerd, and Amy Carmichael. Enrich your life and spiritual journey through these examples of living faith.

Books may be purchased through authors' ministries, online booksellers (Amazon.com, Christianbook.com), and your local Christian bookstore.

A Passion for Prayer: Experiencing Deeper Intimacy with God

Tom Elliff (Christian Literature Crusade, 2010)

PRAYER: What a glorious calling is ours: to pray, to keep praying, and to pray passionately—to persevere in communication with God until we have the assurance God is answering and is working in the situation about which you prayed. A biblical, practical, and thorough primer on the disciplines, challenges, and principles of prayer, all to develop and deepen your communion with God.

Courageous Living: Dare to Take a Stand
Michael Catt (B&H Books, 2011)

CHRISTIAN LIVING: The executive producer of the films *Courageous* and *Fireproof*. Catt takes a closer look at biblical themes and characters who displayed great courage when it would have been easier to play it safe—thus challenging us to courageously keep moving forward through life's trials. Catch a new wind of bravery from the bold accounts of Abraham, Moses, Nehemiah, Ruth, Joshua, Isaiah, Stephen, Paul, and Timothy. Examine your priorities, and deal with anything that brings fear to your heart. And remember to tell everyone to see the movie.

Don't Just Stand There, Pray Something: The Incredible Power of Intercessory Prayer
Ronald Dunn (Thomas Nelson, 1992)

PRAYER: Prayer changes things—and us! An eye-opening book that dispels the myth that only "super-saints" can pray successfully, and describes how anyone—ordained or lay, new Christian or old, full of faith or hesitant—can pray with more purpose and power. A true classic by a seasoned Bible teacher.

Fresh Faith: What Happens When Real Faith Ignites God's People
Jim Cymbala (Zondervan, 1999)

CHRISTIAN LIVING, REVIVAL: Cymbala calls us back to the fiery, passionate preoccupation with God that will restore what the enemy has stolen from us: our first love for Jesus, our zeal, our children, our marriages, and unity in our churches. Born out of the heart and soul of the Brooklyn Tabernacle, the message is illustrated by true stories of men and women whose lives have been changed through the power of faith. Includes a chapter-by-chapter study guide for personal reflection and small group study.

Fresh Wind, Fresh Fire: What Happens When God's Spirit Invades the Hearts of His People
Jim Cymbala (Zondervan, 1997)

CHRISTIAN LIVING, REVIVAL: Cymbala knows firsthand the transforming power of God's love—strong enough to convert prostitutes, pimps, drug addicts, and homeless people. Strong enough to rekindle our own dull hearts and flagging spirits. Experience an example of the New Testament church. You will never be the same.

Heart–Cry for Revival

Stephen Olford (Christian Focus, 2005)

REVIVAL: "Never was a church-wide, heaven-sent revival needed more than at this present time." Every chapter begins with a revival account from Scripture, followed by glimpses into the great revivals of the past three hundred years. Known as the "Preacher's Preacher," Dr. Olford influenced thousands of preachers with his bold appeal to embrace the Lord's call to service and to allow the Holy Spirit to empower that service.

How to Be a World-Class Christian: Becoming Part of God's Global Kingdom

Paul Borthwick (Authentic Media, 2009)

CHRISTIAN SERVICE: God invites you to participate in the greatest, largest, most diverse, and most significant cause in history—His kingdom. A world-class Christian is one whose lifestyle and obedience are compatible with what God is doing in the world. Find and fill the place God has designed for you by using the practical tools, resources, and guiding discussion questions.

Humility: True Greatness

C. J. Mahaney (Multnomah, 2005)

CHRISTIAN LIVING: Mahaney paints a striking picture of the daily battle quietly raging within every Christian and asks if you will passively accommodate pride (the enemy of your soul) or actively cultivate humility (your best friend). When you acknowledge the deception of pride and intentionally humble yourself, you then become free to savor abundant mercies and unlikely graces. Chapters include "The Promise of Humility," "Greatness Redefined," "Identifying Evidences of Grace," "Encouraging Others," "Inviting and Pursuing Correction," "Responding Humbly to Trials," and "A Legacy of Greatness."

Living the Cross Centered Life: Keeping the Gospel the Main Thing
C. J. Mahaney (Multnomah, 2006)

FOUNDATIONS, CHRISTIAN LIVING: What really matters? Have the extremities taken over, leaving the core of your faith forgotten? Then strip away the non-essentials and come back to the simplest, most fundamental reason for our faith: Jesus Christ. Packed with powerful truths that will grip your heart, clear your mind, and invigorate your soul. Chapters include "Breaking the Rules of Legalism," "The Cross Centered Life," "Assurance and Joy."

Not a Fan: Becoming a Completely Committed Follower of Jesus
Kyle Idleman (Zondervan, 2011)

CHRISTIAN LIVING: Are you a fully devoted follower of Jesus, or just a fan who admires Jesus? Some don't yet know what they've said yes to; others don't realize what they've said no to. Idleman invites us to live the way Jesus lived, love the way He loved, pray the way He prayed, and never give up living for the One who gave His all for you. Insightful chapters include "Knowledge About Him or Intimacy with Him?" "Following Jesus or Following the Rules?" "Self-Empowered or Spirit-Filled?" "Come After Me—A Passionate Pursuit," and "Take Up Your Cross Daily—An Everyday Death."

Putting a Face on Grace: Living a Life Worth Passing On
Richard Blackaby (Multnomah Publishers, 2006)

CHRISTIAN LIVING: Blackaby explores what it means to make God's grace a lifestyle. Discover what grace is and what it is not, the power of life words and the destruction of death words, the secret to establishing a grace-filled home, how to recognize grace-giving opportunities, and ways to extend grace when you think you can't. Unable to deny His unconditional love, soon grace will have a face—and the reflection in the mirror will tell your story!

Radical: Taking Back Your Faith from the American Dream
David Platt (Multnomah Publishers, 2010)

CHRISTIAN LIVING, REVIVAL: What is Jesus worth to you? It's easy for American Christians to forget how Jesus said His followers would actually live. They would, He said, abandon everything for the gospel.

Platt invites us to believe and obey what we've heard, and he urges us to join the Radical Experiment—a one-year journey in authentic discipleship that will transform how we live in a world that desperately needs the good news Jesus came to bring.

Streams in the Desert: 366 Daily Devotional Readings (contemporary version)
L. B. Cowan, James Reimann, ed. (Zondervan, 1997)
DEVOTIONAL: Written from the soulful depths of her own trials, Cowan leads us to see that great pressure means great power. Filled with insight into the richness of God's provision and the purpose of His plan, this enduring classic has long sustained and replenished God's weary desert travelers.

The 7 Most Important Questions You'll Ever Answer: Sparking Daily Renewal by Defining the Issues that Really Matter
Daniel Henderson (Strategic Renewal International, 1998)
FOUNDATIONS, CHRISTIAN SERVICE: These practical, humorous, and biblically grounded chapters will challenge you to frame your life around these questions: Who is God? Who am I? What really matters? What should I do? How should I do it? When should I do it? Study questions aid your personal exploration. Don't take another Christian step without reading this book! Revolutionary as a church-wide study.

The Broken Curse
Tom Elliff (Living in the Word Publications, 2009)
CHRISTIAN LIVING: It's difficult to walk in muddy shoes. Are you weighed down with the accumulated failures, disappointments, and verbal clods of the past? Through his personal story, Elliff shares from James 3:9 how to remove the verbal debris that has accumulated on your soul. Experience what it means to run again.

The "B" Series
Warren W. Wiersbe (David C. Cook)
REFERENCE, BIBLE STUDY: Study the Bible in easy-to-read sections that emphasize personal application and biblical meaning. Exciting truths of Scripture wrapped in the warm, personal wisdom of one of America's

best-known Bible teachers. Some titles are *Be Complete* (Colossians), *Be Joyful* (Philippians), *Be Loyal* (Matthew), *Be Mature* (James), *Be Victorious* (Revelation), *Be Resolute* (Daniel), *Be Confident* (Hebrews).

The Complete Works of E. M. Bounds on Prayer: Experience the Wonders of God through Prayer (contemporary version)

E. M. Bounds (compiled by Baker Books, 1990)

PRAYER: This Civil War army chaplain followed the charge to pray without ceasing, and generations of believers have energized their prayer lives with the help of this godly man. Chapters include "The Necessity of Prayer," "The Essentials of Prayer," "The Possibilities of Prayer," "The Reality of Prayer," "Purpose in Prayer," "The Weapon of Prayer," "Power Through Prayer," and "Prayer and Praying Men."

The Green Letters: Principles of Spiritual Growth

Miles J. Stanford (Zondervan, 1975)

FOUNDATIONS, CHRISTIAN LIVING: Perhaps the greatest drama in the world is the slow and subtle growth of character in the Christian. The Christian life is a healthy, robust life. It advances through trials, for in one who has faith even suffering is not wasted, but becomes a means for increasing spiritual vigor and strength. "Not I, but Christ" is its theme.

The Knowledge of the Holy: The Attributes of God: Their Meaning in the Christian Life

A. W. Tozer (HarperCollins, 1961)

FOUNDATIONS: What is the nature of God, and how can we recapture a real sense of God's majesty and truly live in the Spirit? This modern classic illuminates God's attributes—from wisdom, to grace, to mercy—and bears eloquent witness to God's majesty and wonder, and the power of God's Spirit in our daily lives.

The Power of Surrender: Breaking Through to Revival

Michael Catt (B&H Books, 2009)

CHRISTIAN LIVING, REVIVAL: In today's sin-sick world, something has to change. The connection between surrender and revival is not new, but rests in every heart that trusts the Reviver and surrenders every ounce of one's being to the control of the Holy Spirit. Catt unpacks